POINT BUSTER

PETER M. N. WOON

POINT BUSTER

*unlock secret travel wealth
from flyer points and miles*

First published globally in 2025 by

wildlife search pty limited

Copyright © Peter Miles Nicholas Woon 2025. All rights reserved.

The right of Peter Miles Nicholas Woon to be identified as author of this work has been asserted by him in accordance with the Moral Rights Act and any other applicable legislation. No part of this book may be reproduced or transmitted by any person or entity in any form or by any means, electronic or mechanical, including photocopying, recording, scanning or by any information storage and retrieval system, without prior permission in writing from the publisher.

Cataloguing-in-publication entry is available from the National Library of Australia http://catalogue.nla.gov.au

Photography and cover design by Peter Miles Nicholas Woon

ISBN 978-1-7640427-2-7 (paperback)

DISCLAIMER

Although the author and publisher have made every reasonable effort to ensure that the information in this book was correct at press time, they do not assume and hereby disclaim any liability to any party for any loss, damage, or disruption caused by errors or omissions, whether such result from negligence, accident, or any other cause. Examples are indicative only, based upon the author's experience, and with no intentional bias in their selection.

All data are approximate and indicative only. Airline loyalty programs change continually and airfares vary greatly. Native currencies were converted to USDs at exchange rates current at the time of writing.

This book represents the personal views and opinions of the author and is based on the author's perspective and interpretation of the subject matter. The publisher and the author do not make any guarantee or other promise as to any results that may be obtained from using its contents. The information provided is not intended to be a source of financial advice. Names and identifying details have been changed to protect the privacy of individuals.

To my father, with thanks for introducing me to airline loyalty programs nearly 40 years ago over lunch one day in New York City

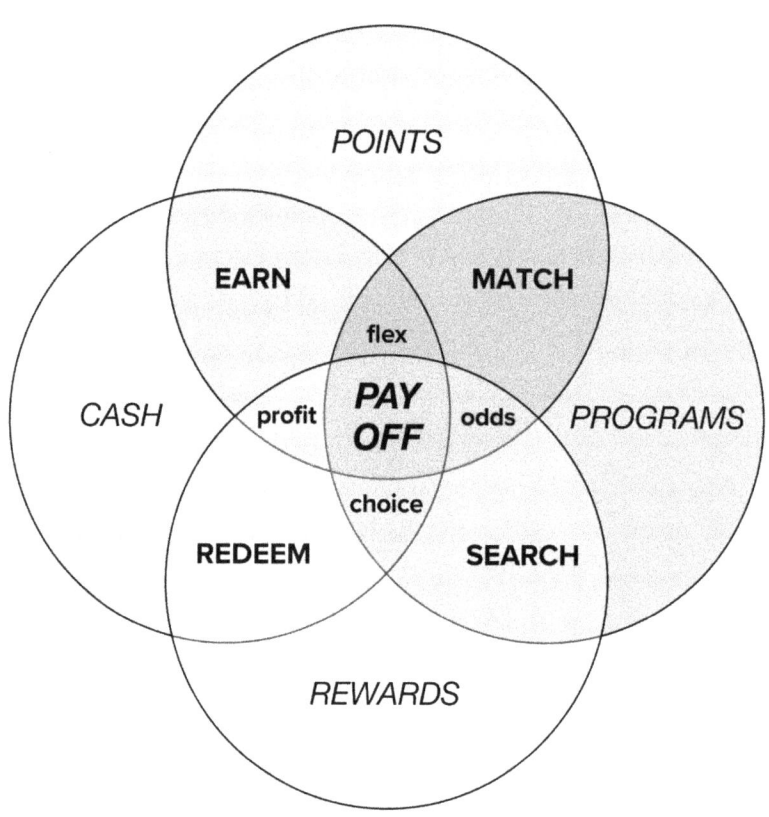

POINT BUSTER

an unauthorized and revolutionary system to supercharge frequent flyer points and miles for travel rich reward

Contents

SEDUCED 1
    Game 4
    Score 7
    Lose 11
    Win 14

GOALS 23
    Cash 26
    Points 33
    Programs 43
    Rewards 52

ACTIONS 61
    Earn 64
    Match 77
    Search 89
    Redeem 100

STRATEGY 115
    Flex 118
    Odds 128
    Choice 139
    Profit 147

PAY-OFF 161
    Juice 165
    Status 174
    Spin 187
    Value 195

SUPERCHARGED 209

    SHOUT-OUT 227
    BIO 229
    STEP UP 231

(Air Tahiti ATR-72 approaching Bora Bora Airport)

SEDUCED TO SUPERCHARGED

SEDUCED

Frequent flyer points literally promise us the world with all of the exciting brilliance of a freshly lit sparkler on a birthday cake. But there's one big problem. They fizzle out fast. We can dutifully earn our points expecting a reward of dream travel, only to find that it all falls apart. We're bedazzled, only to be left with very little or a big fat nothing. We've been seduced by points.

Does any of this sound familiar to you? Signing up to an airline loyalty program, but not knowing what to do next. Earning points, but never having enough for a reward. Searching out reward seats only to discover that most require vast numbers of points. Playing catch up as programs periodically increase the points needed for our dream reward.

And then finally failing to find an affordable reward, because it's in short supply and another one of the many millions of competing players snatched it up first.

Even if we do redeem our points, we can have no idea how well that we've been rewarded for our loyal spend. And that means that we're blind to the biggest secret of the flyer point universe that's hiding in plain sight.

Our flyer points don't have fixed value like the cash in our wallets. They are dynamic and can range from a trickle, delivering a trivial return, to sensational jet set sizzle offering up travel rich reward.

Let's put that another way. Imagine that two customers spend USD1000 in a shop. One receives the reward of a credit voucher for just USD5 and the other for any amount up to USD5000 off the retail price of a future purchase.

That might sound extraordinary, but it illustrates what can happen when we spend cash and earn and then redeem flyer points. With the right process coal dust can be turned into diamonds. Sometimes our flyer points have the potential to be supercharged by up to 1000 times or even greater.

But there's more. Remarkably, the frequent spender is the new frequent flyer. Whether a frequent flyer or not, we can still earn flyer points from the cash that we'd be spending anyway on our day-to-day personal, household, and business expenses. We can enjoy travel rich reward by empowering our everyday spend.

My father slurped his soup noisily, whilst we ate lunch in a modest Chinese restaurant, hidden in a laneway in the Bowery, New York City.

"I didn't pay for your flight! It was free!" He declared.

He had booked me into economy-coach from London to New York on a young Virgin Atlantic. The airline only had two aircraft back in 1987. You have to start somewhere.

Dad's colleague was on my flight, but secluded in *Upper Class*. I went to the front of the Boeing B747, called **Maiden Voyager**, to search him out, but the cabin crew wouldn't let me through and fetched him to meet me for a dismissive handshake.

He slipped back into the unseen world of luxury travel and I retreated back to the cramped reality of economy-coach, embarrassed by his cursory brush-off.

"How did you manage that?" I asked my father.

"It's a new thing they do at Virgin Atlantic, the company bought my return *Upper Class* ticket and I get one return economy-coach ticket for free."

I was stunned that such travel could be free. My only prior experience of loyalty programs was sticking Green Shield Stamps from the local supermarket dutifully into the pages of a book. There were never enough for a reward.

"And there's this thing the airlines do these days to secure your business. Sign up with the airline and collect the points. Redeem the points and get the unused seats for free! You'll thank me one day!" Dad declared. Luckily, for once, I actually listened to the old man. It changed my life and this book is my thanks.

It's finally time to transform from seduced to supercharged, from loser to winner, and go for miles. I'm about to show you how to supercharge your points, but please don't tell anyone, because it's all one big secret.

JUST LIVE IT: play to win

(Air Europa Boeing B787 Dreamliner, Madrid-Barajas Airport)

GO FOR MILES

POINT BUSTER

Game

Being travel rich is ultimately about the experience. We can enjoy meeting new people and reconnecting with far flung family and friends, be inspired by local arts, cuisine, and culture, and be excited to experience the natural environment, or a new adventure or city. Spoiler alert – to do that using flyer points, players need to learn how to outsmart a sophisticated multi-billion-dollar gig, which I call the ***flyer point game***.

It appears to be so easy. To become a player, we simply sign up as a member of an airline loyalty program on the airline's website, usually for free. Then we can earn points across a whole range of everyday personal, household, and business spend, or simply flash certain credit cards, when buying all sorts of stuff from airfares to pharmacy. Once we've saved enough flyer points, we can redeem them for a reward, be that merchandise, travel, or seats on a plane.

But it isn't that easy at all. The stats reveal the confronting truth. Hundreds of millions of us globally have signed up to become members of one or more of the 200 plus airline loyalty programs, only for us to mess it up. A September 2019 survey for Bankrate found that 46 percent of respondents had let their airline and hotel points expire.

Players are sitting on an estimated 30 trillion flyer points globally according to the 2018 McKinsey & Company report, *"Miles Ahead"*. If they were able to redeem all of them at a very modest one US Cent redeemed value per point, then they'd enjoy rewards worth a potential USD300 billion in redeemed value.

But the same report claims between 15 to 30 percent of points expire unused. Players are trashing trillions of points and potentially tens of billions of USDs of redeemed value.

The flyer point game has losers, players who are quite simply left behind, or only ever receive a reward of relatively very poor redeemed value compared with the cash spent earning flyer points. Their points are as under charged and annoying as a flat battery.

I meet people all the time who are misfiring with their flyer points. But what I've discovered is that it's not typically their fault. They stumble because they lack a system to transform their travel dreams into their lived reality.

I've been a player myself for several decades, but never seen a readily available and math-savvy system to play the flyer point game. That's despite the abundant detailed information available on numerous travel blogs. Let's fix that, right here, right now.

Luckily, the flyer point game also has winners. There are players traveling the world in business and first class thanks to flyer points leveraged from their personal, household, and business spend. Their points are supercharged. How do they do it? I'm about to reveal the actions and strategies that can transform our gameplay from that of a loser into that of a winner.

The bad news is that players can already be mentally blocked by their own emotional responses and perceptions. They likely don't even realize that they're being played as puppets in a game of secret seduction by, arguably, the most sophisticated and successful marketing gambits ever invented.

POINT BUSTER

The good news is that we can turn that all around. Our points can be supercharged. And I'm going to share my personal proven playbook to outwit the flyer point game. I call it the POINT BUSTER.

JUST LIVE IT: be a point buster

(Spanish wedding fiesta, Santa Cruz de Tenerife)

EXPERIENCE PEOPLE

Score

Strong points or weak points. Travel rich or travel poor. It's time to make our choice. I'm about to expose the stark difference between winning and losing the flyer point game using one simple number.

People are insanely attracted to points and sign up to loyalty programs in the tens of millions. Extraordinarily, some players receive staggeringly richer travel wealth than others as their reward for a similar loyal spend earning points.

Spoiler alert - we can score our gameplay. We accept that it's sensible to know the annual growth of our superannuation fund, the profit in our business, or the capital gain on our property.

These are all easily measured in one objective math sassy number, a gain, or net return, expressed as a percentage of our starting amount. So why not the net return on our loyalty? The brutal reality is that this gig isn't easy, in fact, it's a rather complicated business.

But the right approach can break down the seemingly difficult into easy steps. Our first task is to adopt a trick used to tackle complex problems by my university supervisor, Professor Vladimir.

We put everything, which we don't understand or want to deal with, into a "black box". Then we simply focus on what we can get out for what we put in.

When we engage with an airline loyalty program, we input cash spent buying stuff that earns points. We output our purchases and a reward in the form of product, which we redeem with those points (see Figure 1).

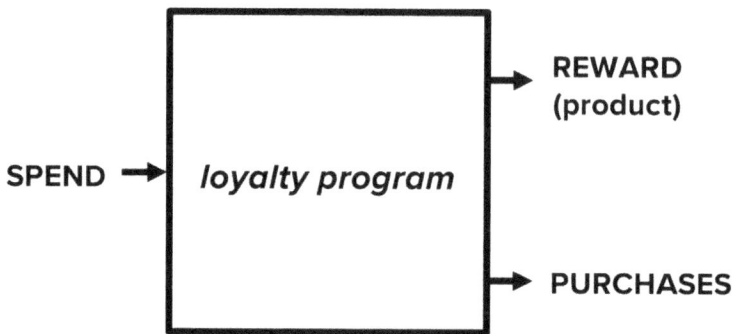

Figure 1: We spend cash and get our purchases and a reward

We know the amount of cash spent buying stuff when earning points. Now let's measure the value of the product redeemed as our reward, be that merchandise or seats on a plane. I've called that **redeemed value** in this book.

Redeemed value differs from **cash**. Our cash is the actual cash sitting in our wallets or bank accounts. We can choose to spend our cash on stuff that earns points.

Redeemed value is basically the equivalent retail cost of our reward when redeeming those points. I recently redeemed points for two one-way first-class flights from Los Angeles to Sydney. The retail cost of those would be about USD10,000. I wasn't rewarded with actual cash in my wallet or bank account when I redeemed my points, rather with product delivering a redeemed value of USD10,000.

I don't consider that I had "saved cash" because I may or may not have paid for those seats in the first place. But I still enjoyed the product, two first-class seats on a plane.

Now we can simply define our objective measure of net return, which I've named the ***Pay-off***. We divide the redeemed value of the reward by our original cash spend and then multiply by 100 to make that a percentage score.

Thus, spending USD1000 cash on stuff that earns points coupled with a reward delivering a redeemed value of USD50, delivers a Pay-off of 50 divided by 1000 and multiplied by 100, which is 5 percent.

Pay-offs can typically range from zero to well over 100 percent, thereby potentially delivering even more in redeemed value than the cash that we spent in the first place.

Calculating the Pay-off reveals that different players can be rewarded with astoundingly different redeemed value for the same cash spend. Amazingly, I'm about to show that in exceptional cases great Pay-off scores can be up to 1000 times or even higher than entry level scores. They can be 500 percent or more, rather than less than one percent. The stark reality is that some players simply get left behind, whilst others go for miles at the front of the aircraft and all for the same loyal spend.

There are broadly three types of players. Some earn points, but never redeem a reward. Their Pay-off is zero. Other players end up with a low Pay-off score because the redeemed value of their reward is small compared with their cash spend. Unless they are spending big cash, they can only go short distances in economy-coach on their points.

And finally, other players secure a great Pay-off score. The redeemed value of their reward is high compared with their cash spend. They have the opportunity to ride in business and first, travel the world, and catch up with family and friends.

The key to finding our own path to success is the irrefutable reality that our *flyer points simply link our cash spend to the redeemed value of our reward*. We need to take control of that relationship to supercharge our points.

Cue the one and only single question that can reveal the true nature of our flyer points. Why is there such a huge variation in Pay-off?

By explaining that, we can exploit the secrets hiding in plain sight to supercharge our points. The bad news is that the answer isn't simple, which may help to explain why some struggle with their flyer points. The good news is that I've already done all of the heavy lifting by crafting the POINT BUSTER.

We can use our Pay-off as an objective measure to guide our gameplay and lend perspective on how we choose to redeem our points to satisfy our own personal travel goals.

JUST LIVE IT: power up the Pay-off

(Virgin Australia Boeing B737)

TRILLIONS OF FLYER POINTS ARE WASTED

Lose

Losing the flyer point game quite simply means being left behind. That can happen when failing to bust through the single biggest barrier standing in our way. And that, in a word, is us. Yes, **us**. Whether realizing it or not, we're all being played in one big psychological mash up of misperceptions, dreams, and emotions. Whether recognizing it or not, we're being secretly seduced by points.

Players each have their personal desire to travel and to experience the people and places of the planet. I like to call that our jet zest. Jet because players aspire to a rapid stream of success through the airline loyalty system to accelerate their path to travel rich reward.

They want wings and to be powered by the miracles of science and technology around the planet at close to the speed of sound. They want to seize the moment, they have things to do, places to visit, and people to meet.

Zest because their dreams inspire their enthusiasm and energy. They want their lives to be more exciting, better expressed, and celebrated with others. They want the taste of their experience to be sharper, their presence keener, and to be their true selves to the very core. They want to turn their travel dreams into their lived reality.

But I strongly suspect that most are unaware of the extent of the psychological and emotional seduction that's at large in the flyer point game. And it's a seduction that's fueled by our individual jet zest as airline loyalty programs use a mirror to reflect our very own personal dreams and desires straight back at us as they scoop up ever more coin.

I was a puppet myself for years. I even know highly intelligent folk with extensive flyer point experience, who are still unwittingly secretly seduced by points.

They trash way too many points on a reward seat because they've missed the memo on how different types of reward can deliver such starkly different redeemed value for their points.

They're so blindly stuck on status that they spend their weekends blowing big cash to fly frivolously around a continent to maintain status for the convenience of a premium phone line and an occasional visit to a first-class lounge.

Consider this. I used to take my dog to enjoy the off-leash area of our local beach when he was still a puppy. The reward of a treat when he came back to me secured his compliant behavior. Good job, he'd become conditioned.

But the day came when the sassy sod called my bluff. He stopped coming back when called. He had figured out that continued freedom was more valuable to him than a hit of dried liver. My little fur baby had done the math and busted the system.

Of course, when we look at ourselves in the mirror, we like to believe that what we see looking back at us is far too smart and sophisticated to be conditioned like our dutiful dog.

Reality check – before you picked up this book, did you believe that your flyer points were free, or did you assume points were like money with a fixed value, or focus on your cash saved rather than redeemed value? If so, no problem, you've simply been a puppet in this game just like the rest of us. We've all been played.

Marketing gurus know how to press our emotional and psychological buttons, from the rush of collecting points to the hit of redeeming a reward. But we can bust any behavioral conditioning by doing the math, just like my puppy.

JUST LIVE IT: *do the math*

(Church of Saint Anthony, Lisbon)

EXPERIENCE CULTURE

Win

Winning the flyer point game simply means that we enjoy travel rich reward. But first, we need to shatter the six seductive powers of our flyer points. Players can be simply unaware that these exist or ill-equipped to outwit them. Winners can spin from challenge to strategic advantage.

Confused to Clear

The flyer point game is opaque. Our Pay-off is hidden. Let's contrast that with visiting the local mall, where we'll see promotions with defined percentage discounts advertised in shop windows. Attractive discounts encourage us to enter the shop and make a purchase.

We are motivated to spend by the instant gratification of paying less than the full retail cost. I recently bought a shirt in an outlet store because it was discounted by 70 percent. I had the information to make my choice.

But in the flyer point game, our cash spend is motivated by the instant gratification of earning points. We still get the hit even though our points aren't actual cash. We save points without a clear understanding of their potential redeemed value or our eventual Pay-off.

Imagine spending USD200 in the local department store and being offered the choice between a voucher for USD2 against a future purchase of product in that store, representing a Pay-off of one percent, or a voucher for USD200, representing a Pay-off of 100 percent. It would be easy to pick out the best deal.

We'd say, yes please to the USD200 voucher and no to the USD2 voucher. Clearly, a Pay-off of 100 percent is more valuable than that of just one percent, regardless of how much cash that we would have been prepared to spend on the originally purchased item in the first place.

But in the airline loyalty gig players are effectively offered a voucher without being told its value. They can end up with a Pay-off of just one percent or less, if they choose based on emotion, or up to 100 percent or more, if they do the math.

Now we can choose to blunder our way through the flyer point game blissfully unaware of our Pay-off and confused about the value of our points. Alternatively, we can adopt an objective and consistent approach and then make informed choices about the options that satisfy our personal travel goals.

Remember, points are highly dynamic. To spin from confused to clear, we need to calculate the Pay-off as a guide to our gameplay and personal choices. I've created the POINT BUSTER to accelerate our Pay-off.

Exposed to Prepared

The flyer point game is risky. Our reward isn't certain. Conversely, some retail shop loyalty programs offer customers an instant discount, say 10 percent off anything that they buy. Customers enjoy the certainty and instant gratification of an immediate discount as they pay at the till.

But in the flyer point game, players receive points for their purchases and redeem those points for a reward at a later date. Their reward is ***deferred***.

POINT BUSTER

Try offering a young child one candy now and tell them that they can have two candies in 15 minutes time, but only if they can resist eating the first candy. That was the basis of the Marshmallow Test run decades ago in Stanford University.

Such delayed gratification is a set up. Loyalty programs can sucker players into that long line of crying children, who couldn't resist the first hit of candy. Players are tempted by the immediate pleasure triggered by the excitement of earning points.

The actual reward isn't a matter of minutes away, but potentially, days, weeks or months, so distant that it can be the player's power of imagination and the temptation of their dreams, that impact their decisions at the time of purchase.

The second aspect of this risky business happens when players come to redeem their points. They face uncertain probability of success. They're not guaranteed the second candy, even if they can summon up the patience to wait it out. There's only a chance that they'll get the reward that they want when they come to redeem their points. Indeed, they may have absolutely no idea of their odds of success.

The third facet of the dicey deal is that some airline loyalty programs have adopted dynamic reward pricing, in which the points needed to redeem a given reward isn't fixed. Players aren't certain where they stand.

Finally, players don't know if and when a program will devalue creating an ever-moving target as the number of points required for their goal reward creeps ever higher.

Now we can choose to accept our lot hoping that somehow it will all work out in the end. Alternatively, we can learn how to take steps to prepare for and manage the risks of the game.

If we want to spin from exposed to prepared, we need to adopt the actions and strategies that empower us to take control of our flyer point destiny. I've based the POINT BUSTER upon proven practical gameplay.

Puppet to Player

Airline loyalty programs are gamified. Members are sucked into playing a game, based upon earning, saving, and redeeming points, whilst inadvertently enticed to spend ever more coin. The more that they engage in any given program, the more points that they can earn.

The airline loyalty program is effectively rewarding their behavior when they perform as intended. The goal is literally to keep members loyal to the one program, to lock them in. Members love to earn and collect points. They can't resist a reward that some wrongly perceive as free. They engage in the game.

But because they're all chasing the same rewards, they're also playing against each other. They're competing for individual success with all of the many millions of other members.

Programs can also rank loyalty through the instrument of status. Members are assigned a tier, such as Bronze, Silver, Gold, or Platinum, based upon the amount of business that they direct through a program's parent airline and partners.

Members have to complete tasks, such as reaching targets of cash spend or flights taken or distance flown. Programs reward compliant behaviors with an increasing array of potentially beneficial features, such as access to airline lounges.

Programs are effectively conditioning their members to lock them into the one program and encourage them to pay relatively higher airfares in the pursuit of status.

Members love the challenge of rising through the ranks of status. And then they have to do it all over again as the targets are reset every year entrapping them into repeating cycles of requalification. And the more that they do it, the ever more conditioned that they can become.

Now we can choose to be a puppet and simply to fall into line and comply with the rules of the game. Alternatively, we can learn how to play the game to win.

To spin from puppet to player, we need to improve our knowledge of the flyer point game. I've collated the essential learning from nearly 40 years as a player myself to define the four circles of the POINT BUSTER and reveal how the parts can be fused together to supercharge our flyer points.

Dream to Reality

The gig is aspirational. Players can easily be enticed by their very own dreams. Just check out the marketing pitch used on an airline website of your choice.

Recurrent motifs cite personal travel dreams and once in a lifetime experiences. One program entices "dream closer" and another promises, "your travel dreams mean the world to us". Imagine relaxing on a tropical island beach, being entranced by a pride of lions on a wildlife safari, or whatever takes your flight of fancy.

We each harbor our travel dreams, no problem, but only if they motivate us to find our path to attain our goals. We don't want to get stuck in the zone of desires that are never fulfilled.

In the movie, *"Inception"*, the characters are jolted awake from their adventures in a dreamscape by being tumbled backwards into a bath of cold water.

As the writer / director, Christopher Nolan, is quoted as saying in IndieWire in part to explain the mind-boggling film, "generally someone says something along the lines of 'chase your dreams', but I don't want to tell you that because I don't believe that, I want you to chase your reality."

Now we can opt to keep dreaming about stuff and accept the self-limiting notion of a once in a lifetime travel event. Alternatively, we can recast our dreams as goals and embrace them as attainable. Some other players are enjoying travel rich reward. It might as well be us.

To spin from our dreams to our lived reality, we need to embrace a proven system. I've crafted the POINT BUSTER as a practical playbook to guide our path to success.

Seduced to Savvy

Points are seductive. Intimate emotional responses are being toyed. When players earn points, they can feel good, because they think that points are free and their loyalty is respected.

A travel dream promises the player a journey to the very people and places of their most private and personal desires. Just thinking about those can be enough to give them a rush through the release of feel-good hormones that attach to the nerve cells in their brains.

When their perceptions and expectations are subject to their subconscious wiring, they can become enraptured by their emotion.

Redeeming their points can stimulate the satisfaction of being able to secure a reward for their loyalty. Players can feel great because they mistakenly believe that they got something for free.

Players can also get trippy with status. Those on higher tiers are branded as elite. They can become one of those special few and feel better and more important than others.

Players have to climb the rising steps of the ladder of status itself to be at the pinnacle of success. Then they have to do it all over again each year. But when they do make it, they can feel recognized, worthy, and important.

Basically, players' egos can become so tied up with the anxiety of continually attaining elite status, making it hard to rationalize their choices and balance the upsides and downsides of chasing airline status.

Now we can opt to succumb to our emotional responses. Alternatively, we can park them and adopt a rationalist and objective approach. We can then make our personal choices with that added perspective. We can still enjoy the ride, have fun, and feel satisfied, but as outcomes of mastering the game.

To spin from seduced to savvy, we need to take the emotion out of the equation and replace it with some basic math. I've anchored the POINT BUSTER to an objective numbers-based approach.

Poor to Rich

Our loyalty has been monetized. The reality is that airline loyalty programs are big business. They make revenue by selling points to program partners, such as credit card companies and retailers, and can be highly profitable.

Players have inadvertently become caught up in a vast flow of cash and a counter flow of points circulating through the loyalty universe. They can easily fail to grasp the size and scope of the gig or its purpose to scoop up coin.

Now we can opt to attach to our perception that points are free, therefore rewards are free and a benevolent gift for our loyalty. Alternatively, we can recognize that this loyalty gig is monetized. It's driven by our cash spend. It's just business.

To spin from travel poor to rich, we need to score our performance in objective cash terms. I've designed the **POINT BUSTER** to empower our everyday spend for travel rich reward.

JUST LIVE IT: kickstart the path

(Qantas Airways Airbus A330, Sydney Airport)

PUPPET TO PLAYER

POINT BUSTER

(Monument to Felipe IV, Madrid)
Success - Bogotá to Madrid
Avianca Business Class
(avianca life**miles**)

GOALS

We're here for travel rich reward. I'm about to set four key goals to get the job done. But first, it's time to start building our math-based system, the POINT BUSTER. As we do, I'll flesh out the essential background knowledge, that we're going to need to play the flyer point game.

Our first step is to draw four overlapping circles. That's it. We can unlock the hidden secrets of how to play the game with just those four circles.

It's tempting to think that there are only two physical elements to consider when engaging with an airline loyalty program.

Our focus is easily drawn to the physical elements of our points and our rewards. Players earn points. When they have saved sufficient points, they can redeem their reward, a product such as merchandise or seats on a plane.

Let's draw our first two overlapping circles and label one **Points** and the other **Rewards**. And for many members of airline loyalty programs, that's simply the end of the matter.

But there's more. The system is driven by cash. Players spend cash on all sorts of stuff supplied by companies who allocate points for their loyal custom within the framework of a given airline loyalty program. So, let's add two more overlapping circles and label one **Cash** and the other **Programs**.

Spoiler alert - the secrets of the game are hiding in the overlaps between those circles. I'll expose four levels of complexity and reveal how we can take control of the game as we systematically build the POINT BUSTER (see Figure 2).

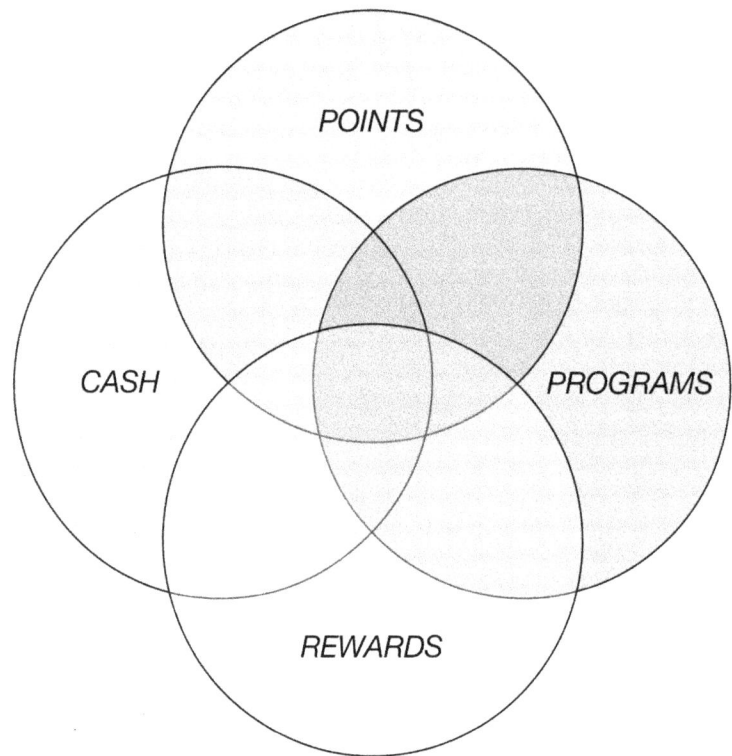

Figure 2: The POINT BUSTER has four overlapping circles

We'll set our goals and targets, whilst building our essential knowledge of the game in book section GOALS. We'll explore winning power packing actions in section ACTIONS. We'll expose how those actions can be strategically combined to boost each other in section STRATEGY. We'll learn how to avoid a hidden trap in section PAY-OFF. And then we'll fuse all of that savvy together to unleash the atomic potential of our flyer points in concluding section SUPERCHARGED.

JUST LIVE IT: be goal driven

GOALS

(Art installation in Venice by Hungarian artist, Vincze Ottó)

CONFUSED TO CLEAR

Cash

Our goal for cash is our headline goal, to empower the everyday cash that we'd be spending anyway to generate travel rich reward.

Let's start with a closer look at the circle of CASH, the first of the four circles of the POINT BUSTER. It represents the cash that we spend that earns the points of any given airline loyalty program (see Figure 3).

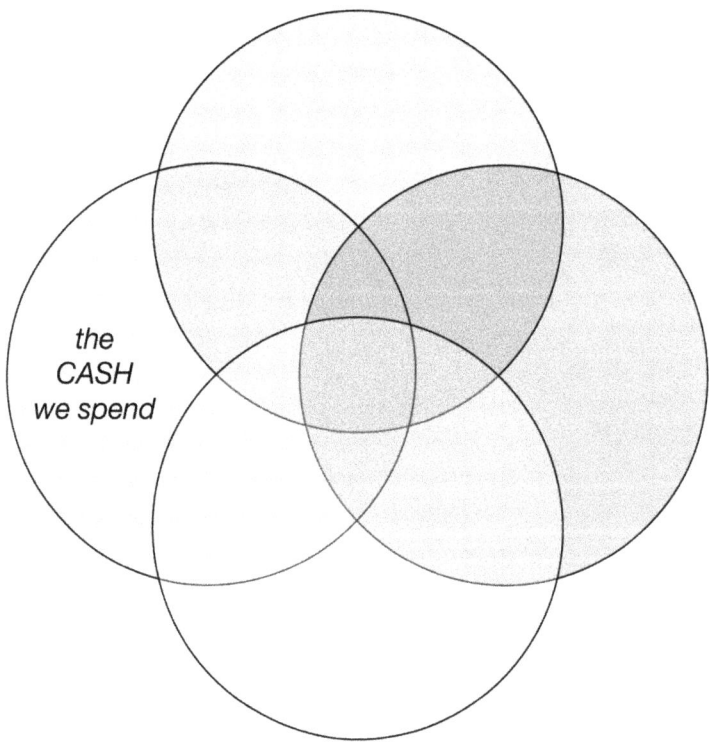

Figure 3: The CASH we spend

It's all about the **cash**. I'm talking money: the cheddar, cabbage and clams, or the moolah, scratch and loot. An airline loyalty program is a business. It succeeds when it generates revenues, secures profits, collects customer data, and forms a valuable asset for the parent airline.

Our own loyal engagement with an airline loyalty program is ultimately a series of financial transactions. They involve ***our cash***. Even with no immediate cash flow out of our wallets, such as receiving bonus points for opening a bank or investment account, there will be a cash price for us to pay, such as transaction fees or relatively less favorable interest rates, as points reward our behaviors now to suck up our coin later.

We can double up when our employer pays for stuff, like our travel expenses. We can earn points on the back of our employer's or our own business cash spend **and** from our personal and household everyday cash spend. In both cases, cash is spent with the parent airline or one of the program partners to earn our points.

In time, the POINT BUSTER will rotate full circle when we redeem our points for our reward. Our reward is in the form of product. We can apply an objective measure of its worth, redeemed value, based upon its retail price. By closing the loop, we end up with our Pay-off, which measures the redeemed value of our reward relative to our original cash spend.

To satisfy our cash goal to empower everyday spend, the POINT BUSTER targets more cash, more product, and higher Pay-offs.

More Cash

We can earn more points with more cash in play. We can amp up our flyer point gameplay to enjoy our reward faster by seizing wide ranging opportunities to earn points that are staring us the face. These include earning points from a huge diversity of everyday spend, be that purchasing fuel or groceries, paying rent or taxes.

Some people assume that you need to be a frequent flyer to play the flyer point game. You don't. Of course, if we do earn points through the purchase of airfares and travel, that's still great, but it's just one potential category of spend that can pump up our points.

Let's check out some stats. It's claimed that 60 percent of flyer points, called Avios, were collected through everyday spend outside of flying by the 2023 *"Capital Markets Day"* report from International Airlines Group (IAG), the parent company for the airlines British Airways, Iberia, Aer Lingus, and Vueling. The everyday spender is the new frequent flyer.

Players can earn points through any of the program partners listed on the website of the parent airline of any given airline loyalty program and their respective online shopping malls.

Additionally, point-earning credit cards can offer a route to earn points from **any** transactions that players make using their cards. Significantly, they don't need to fly or spend with a program or its partners.

Basically, we can be a frequent flyer, or frequent spender, or even both. We can extend the scope of our gameplay. We can target more cash.

More Product

In the flyer point game, we spend cash, get the stuff that we've just bought and also earn points to redeem later for a reward. We're not rewarded with cash, but product, such as merchandise or seats on a plane.

Obviously, this is different to, say, investing cash in a savings account, or trying to pump up the bucks by flipping a property or playing the stock market. In such cases, we can end up with additional cold hard cash when we choose wisely.

Although players don't accrue actual cash, they can get close to it, since some airline loyalty programs offer the facility to redeem points for gift vouchers. But they can only spend the gift voucher in certain stores or situations.

Now players might go ahead and try and assign some sort of value to their reward, the product received. I've done that objectively in this book by using the retail value of the reward to calculate redeemed value.

Some players do so subjectively. Thus, they might consider what they would've been prepared to pay for the redeemed item or potential savings against a personal travel budget. But they still haven't returned any actual cold hard cash.

Basically, enjoying greater reward means receiving more product for our flyer points. We can target more product.

Higher Pay-offs

We can seek a higher Pay-off, more product per buck spent. There's opportunity to extract more travel rich reward.

Let's check out the basics of loyalty marketing. Firstly, let's consider a loyalty program with a ***fixed Pay-off***, in which everyone gets the same reward back for the same loyal spend.

POINT BUSTER

My local café has a small yellow card that gets stamped whenever a customer buys a coffee. After buying nine coffees the customer can enjoy one, which they believe is free. And we're all suckers for something that we think is free.

If the retail price of the coffee is USD3.00, the customer pays USD27.00 for nine coffees and then gets one at no further cost. They get a reward in coffee, but not actual cash. They might feel that they've saved USD3.00, but their reward is in the form of product, in this case coffee.

The USD3.00 retail price of that coffee provides an objective measure of how much their reward is worth. They have accrued USD3.00 in *redeemed value*. Their Pay-off is fixed at 3 divided by 27 times 100, or about 11 percent.

By contrast most airline loyalty programs present a *variable Pay-off*. Members don't all get the same back for the same loyal spend.

Let's check out an example. We all buy groceries as part of our everyday spend and some of us can earn points for doing just that depending upon the airline loyalty program.

I earn Flybuys points when I shop at a Coles supermarket. Then I transfer those points to Velocity, the airline loyalty program of Virgin Australia Airlines. I receive an email from Flybuys each year summarizing my annual performance.

A tasty pie-chart shows that I have consistently earned ten times more bonus points than base points by clicking the *activate offer* link in their emails to accept a dance of bonus points for ever increasing spend targets.

The rate at which I can earn my Flybuys points per dollar isn't fixed. The system seeks to drive my purchasing behaviors by promising bonus points to entice higher spend.

But the emails don't cite a Pay-off score. So, I calculated that for myself and a couple of friends. Sal runs our local Italian trattoria. He returned USD5 credit against a future grocery purchase for every USD1000 spent, a Pay-off of 0.5 percent.

By contrast, Michaela from our local gym activated her bonus offers and still used her points as a credit against the cost of her groceries. She returned USD50 credit for every USD1000 spent. Her Pay-off was 5 percent, but still *10 times* better than Sal's.

I returned USD650 redeemed value for every USD1000 spent by transferring my points to Virgin Airlines Velocity and then redeeming them for business class reward seats. That delivered a Pay-off of about 65 percent, *13 times* higher than Michaela's and *130 times* higher than Sal's.

Incidentally, I also collect Everyday Rewards points when I shop at Woolworths, supermarkets and transfer the points to Qantas Airways Qantas Frequent Flyer.

Significantly, both Sal and Michaela can easily elevate their Pay-off through small changes in their actions. The exact opportunities obviously depend upon where we live and with which loyalty programs we engage.

Let's check out an example of a rare opportunity unleashing an exceptional Pay-off. In 2021, my small business spent about USD700 on fuel during a promotion for bonus Qantas Frequent Flyer points.

Those points were later redeemed for flights from Barcelona to London and onto Los Angeles in business and first class respectively, on British Airways. The points returned approximately USD6300 in redeemed value.

POINT BUSTER

In this case, my Pay-off was about 900 percent. I was getting *nine times* more back in redeemed value than my business spent on the fuel and *1800 times* higher Pay-off than the base Pay-off of 0.5 percent for that particular frequent flyer program.

Basically, the redeemed value that we can get back for the same loyal spend varies hugely. We can target higher Pay-offs.

JUST LIVE IT: empower everyday spend

(Circular Quay, Sydney)

Success - Los Angeles to Sydney
Qantas First Class (Qantas Frequent Flyer)

Points

Our goal for points is to supercharge our flyer points. Let's take a closer look at what lies within the second of the four circles in the POINT BUSTER. The circle of POINTS represents the points that we earn through any given airline loyalty program (see Figure 4).

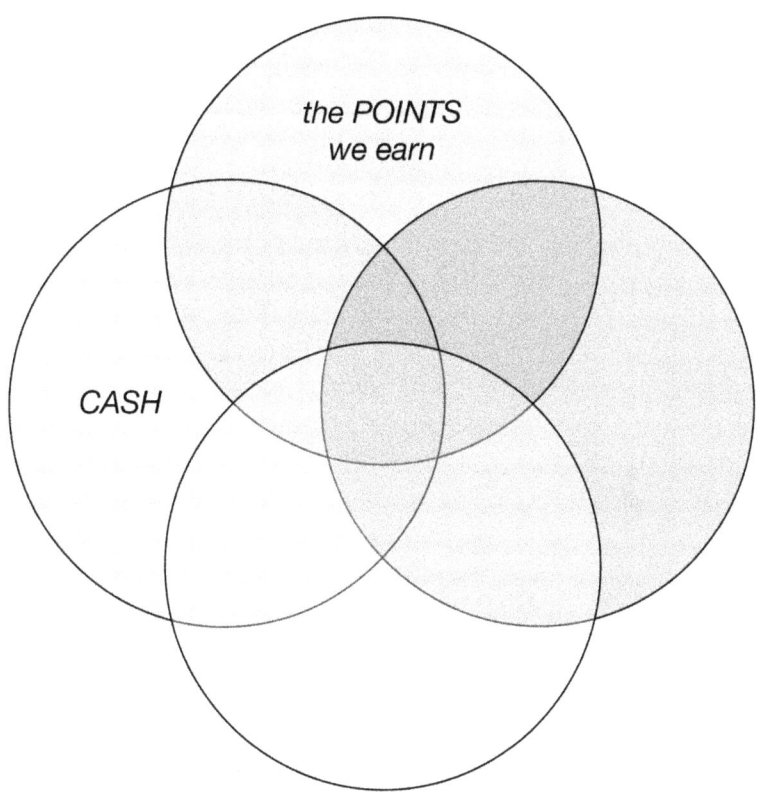

Figure 4: The POINTS we earn

Points are simply the tokens of loyalty circulating through all airline loyalty programs. They bridge our cash spend to our reward.

Other examples of loyalty tokens, include those ten circles on a card, which are stamped every time a customer buys a coffee, those earned through hotel and shopping loyalty programs, and through spend on some credit cards.

Typically, each airline loyalty program issues its own loyalty tokens. To cite a few of the dozens, members earn the miles of United MileagePlus, of avianca life**miles**, and of Etihad Guest. Likewise, the points of Virgin Atlantic Flying Club, of Air Canada Aeroplan, and of Qantas Frequent Flyer.

For perspective, the *"Qantas Annual Report 2024"* claims that the 16.4 million members of Qantas Frequent Flyer earned 202 billion points in the 2024 financial year.

Some programs call their loyalty tokens miles because traditionally the tokens earned can be calculated based upon miles flown when members buy and fly with an airline. I've called them all points, unless referring to a specific loyalty currency, which uses miles or a different name.

Now if you believe that points are free, you're not alone. But points aren't free. Earn or leave them, redeem or ignore them, points are ultimately bankrolled by the consumer. That means that they were either paid for by ourselves or our employers, when we buy airfares and other stuff and pay credit card fees and less favorable interest rates, and so forth.

Let's go back to that café, because it presents a simple way to illustrate the concept. The café owner charges USD3.00 for one coffee, but the actual cost of supply is less than that, let's assume USD2.70.

The cost of supply of the reward, the tenth coffee, can be spread across the revenue from selling nine coffees at the retail price of USD3.00.

The café owner only needs to allocate USD0.30 for each of the nine coffees sold to offset the USD2.70 cost of supply of the reward, some 10 percent of revenue from coffee sales.

The café owner incurs a marketing expense as part of that USD2.70 cost of supply per coffee, with the goal of keeping their customers loyal.

Spoiler alert – the tenth coffee isn't free at all. The customer paid for nine coffees in the first place. If the business owner has done their math, then the marketing cost has already been factored into the cost of supply and thereby the retail cost of the coffees that customers purchase.

When we buy airfares, the cost-benefit of allocating points and then delivering rewards has been factored into the retail price of airfares.

Similarly, the various program partners have calculated the cost-benefit of purchasing points from the program and then allocating points to us when we spend our cash. They've factored all of that into the retail price with the goal of retaining our business and upping our loyal cash spend.

Basically, our points simply link our loyal spend to our reward. To satisfy our points goal to supercharge our flyer points, the **POINT BUSTER** targets more points, more bang for buck, and greater flexibility.

More Points

In our simple café scenario, customers receive one loyalty token for each coffee purchased. Assuming each coffee costs the same, they're earning loyalty tokens at a constant rate. They're getting the same number of loyalty tokens per dollar.

But airline loyalty programs are typically different. The number of points that members can earn for each dollar spent can vary enormously depending upon the situation.

In some cases, members receive a nominated number of points per dollar spend. For example, there's a trend for airline loyalty programs to calculate points earned from flying based upon the amount paid for the airfare rather than distance flown. Thus, members currently earn 5 AAdvantage miles per USD spent on airfares with program parent airline American Airlines, or more, if they have status in that program.

Carriers of a credit card, which earns points, also accrue a set number of points per dollar spent on the card, although this can vary depending upon the category of spend, for example, be different for travel expenses, or restaurant meals, or groceries.

The points earned per dollar spend can vary enormously as program partners seek to entice and lock in our business. For example, I can earn just one or two points per dollar shopping for groceries and retail goods, or many times that, even up to 300 points per dollar in exceptional cases, when there are offers of bonus points.

Basically, the huge variation in how many points we can earn per dollar spend creates an opportunity to accrue many more points and do that faster. We can target more points.

More Bang for Buck

We can enjoy more reward per point. Our flyer points are dynamic. Their value isn't fixed. That clears a path for us to unleash relatively greater redeemed value when the time comes to redeem our flyer points.

Sometimes flyer points are described as currencies. That makes some sense from the perspective of the airline loyalty program. Programs sell points to their program partners. They match the required number of points to the cost of purchasing a reward to supply to the member, effectively buying back the points when they are redeemed.

But our points are not a traditional cash currency. Governments do not issue them like New Zealand Dollars, Colombian Pesos, and British Pounds.

Some airline loyalty programs present the opportunity to purchase flyer points with cash. Even then, we can't exchange our flyer points back to cash.

Apart from some exceptions, our points are not legally considered to be a cash equivalent. They don't tend to come under local financial regulations controlling the money of a given country.

The good news is that we typically don't have to pay tax on our points. The bad news is that airline loyalty programs can sit outside of financial laws and regulations, although potentially subject to local consumer and data protection laws.

Airline loyalty programs thereby have a degree of freedom about how they go about their business and can easily change the aspects of the program, such as the number of points we need to redeem for a given reward.

POINT BUSTER

If we think of flyer points as cash currencies, we risk being diverted away from their dynamic nature. Unlike our flyer points, units from the same cash currency always have the same buying power. Ten bucks in our wallet has the same buying power as ten bucks in somebody else's wallet.

But flyer points from different and even the same airline loyalty programs typically don't have a fixed value. This reality can be surprising, if we assume up front that points are similar to our cash where one Japanese Yen is always a Japanese Yen and one United Arab Emirates Dirham is always one United Arab Emirates Dirham, and so forth.

In the flyer game, players aren't rewarded with cash, but rather with product, such as merchandise, hotel rooms, or seats on a plane. In this book, we measure the value of the reward objectively as redeemed value.

Now let's expose the great variation in the redeemed value of our points. Sooner or later, players want to know how much their points are worth. I currently have 850,000 Qantas Frequent Flyer points. What's their value?

We can get a feel for a minimum potential redeemed value of our points by seeing how many are required for a gift voucher or item of merchandise. In such cases, Qantas Frequent Flyer points have a redeemed value of about USD3.50 for every 1000 points when redeemed. My stash of 850,000 points is then potentially worth about USD2975 in redeemed value.

I researched one-way business class reward seats from Sydney to Johannesburg. The potential redeemed value was USD40 for every 1000 points. Now my stash of points is potentially worth up to USD34,000 in redeemed value.

Extraordinarily, there's an approximately 11 times variation in the potential redeemed value of my stash of points in these specific examples.

Remember that I don't have that amount of cash sitting in an account, because my reward will be in product. The redeemed value depends upon our choice of reward.

Our perceptions of value can also impact our gameplay. Some players like to consider the cash that they would have otherwise spent on the reward that they plan to redeem with their points. That can shift their focus away from redeemed value to the cash that they believe that we can save by redeeming their points.

But we need to be careful not to fall into that secret seduction perfected by the brilliant marketing gambits of airline loyalty programs. Let's work through a hypothetical scenario.

Imagine a player with a budget of USD850 for a one-way flight from Sydney to Johannesburg on Qantas Airways. A typical economy airfare of USD850 is bang on budget.

But now let's assume that they have ample Qantas Frequent Flyer points. They can choose to redeem a batch of points rather than pay for the airfare. Once they've paid the cash co-payment of USD125 that's required for the reward, they're up USD725. They can view that as a saving of USD725 over the cash that they'd have spent on the airfare. They now have USD725 of their original budget left over to spend on something else

That sounds great. But hold on a minute. When they focus on their USD850 budget, they risk bypassing the option to redeem their points for a flight in another cabin class.

Such options aren't even on their personal radar, because the retail airfares for premium economy, business, and first class all cost a lot more than their nominated cash budget.

Even if they are, the saving would be capped at the value of their personally nominated budget. And then, their apparent cash savings would shift, if they simply adjusted their budget.

By simply nominating a higher budget, they could conclude that they've saved more cash by using their points. In short, perceptions of cash saved are entirely subjective.

What are we missing? By redeeming our flyer points, we get product, not cash. We risk missing the opportunity to secure more product for our original cash spend, when focusing ***solely*** on a perception of cash saved.

In our example above, a player also has the choice of redeeming their points for other cabin classes. If they opt for business class, they enjoy a product with a retail value of USD3750 and a markedly richer travel experience.

Once they'd paid the reward cash co-payment, they'd still have about USD660 of their originally nominated budget left over to spend on something else. They'd ***also*** get more product, thus ***more bang for buck***.

We can assess the worth of the product, our reward, in two ways, objectively, based upon redeemed value, and subjectively, for example, based upon perceptions of cash saved. Of course, there is a third option, to consider ***both*** approaches to guide our choices when redeeming our points.

We can enjoy our reward regardless of whether we would have paid cash for that reward, and irrespective of our personal budget, and whatever our financial wealth.

Basically, we can favor those rewards that unlock relatively more redeemed value for our points. We can target more bang for buck.

Greater Flexibility

We're about to discover that flexibility in how we allocate our flyer points across multiple airline loyalty programs is one key to unlock their potential to deliver travel rich reward.

Roadblock - typically we can't exchange our flyer points directly between airline loyalty programs. The practical reality is that we have to commit to the one airline loyalty program, when we spend cash and accrue flyer points. We have to decide how to allocate our points as they are earned.

We can still engage with a number of partner airlines through the one program. Thus, we can earn and redeem Etihad Guest miles when flying on Air France or KLM, because they are partner airlines of Etihad Guest. Similarly, we can earn or redeem miles of Flying Blue, the airline loyalty program of Air France and KLM, when flying on Etihad.

But we can't transfer miles between our Etihad Guest account and our Flying Blue account. There are a few exceptional cases, which we'll learn how to exploit later in chapter MATCH.

Fortunately, loyalty tokens used by certain ***program partners*** can be converted into flyer points. These include certain generic credit cards. These products allow us to accrue points offered by the card-issuing company, such as American Express, Capital One, and Citibank, to name a few, and then convert them to certain airline loyalty program points later as needed to redeem for a reward. This empowers flexibility.

Hotel chains also have loyalty programs, which enable members to earn points for paid accommodation. Some hotel loyalty points can be transferred into various airline loyalty program accounts.

There are also other retail loyalty programs, which interface with an airline loyalty program. For example, in the UK, players can earn Nectar points when spending with 500 brands and then transfer them into British Airways Club Avios.

Basically, despite limited capacity to exchange our flyer points, we can still earn and group them strategically. We can still target greater flexibility.

JUST LIVE IT: fortify flyer points

(Interstate 10, Los Angeles)

Success – London to Los Angeles
British Airways First Class
(Alaska Airlines Mileage Plan)

Programs

Our goal for programs is to select those airline loyalty programs that can work best for us. We're after better opportunity to earn and redeem our points. Let's take a closer look at what lies within the third of circle of the POINT BUSTER. The circle of PROGRAMS represents the airline loyalty programs that we choose (see Figure 5).

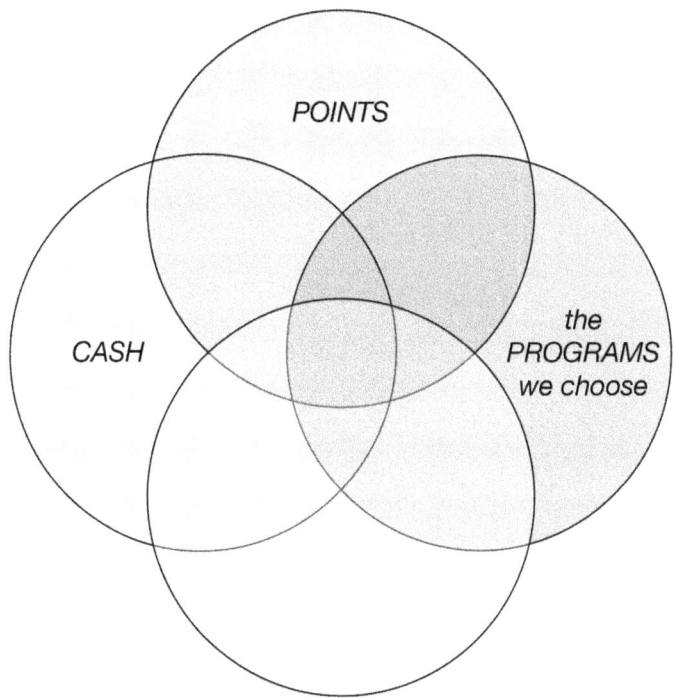

Figure 5: The PROGRAMS we choose

Airline loyalty programs are brilliant global marketing gigs, if not the most exceptional of modern times. They've been around for about 45 years and now they are over 200.

There are also three established major airline alliances, called Star Alliance, **one**world, and SkyTeam, in which a number of airlines form agreements to extend their reach.

Players only need to be a member of one of the allied airline's respective loyalty programs to earn and redeem points for reward seats across other alliance airlines, depending upon how well reward seats are made available between allied airlines.

Members with status in one program can also benefit from some status tier features across that program's allied airlines.

Some airlines don't belong to one of the big three alliances, but still set up a network of airline partners. Thus, Emirates Skywards partners with about 15 airlines.

To satisfy our programs goal to select those frequent flyer programs that work best for us, the POINT BUSTER targets wiser loyalty, more programs, and better fit.

Wiser Loyalty

Loyalty is a two-way street, right? Well, yes, when we're talking about our relationships with our friends and partners. But not necessarily with a business. We don't have a mutually loving feel-good relationship with a corporate entity. Blind loyalty can misdirect our gameplay.

Airline loyalty is all about locking in our business and we need to assess the merits of our engagement objectively by taking the emotion out of the equation and doing the math.

I've already unpacked how players can be secretly seduced, so that they can become locked in by their emotional and psychological responses. Now let's explore how airline loyalty programs are designed to scoop up coin. It's just business.

Let's continue to strip down what's happening behind the scenes of typical loyalty programs by building a highly simplified and hypothetical model of a modern airline loyalty program. I've called it the Jet Zest Airlines Loyalty program, or just **Program** for short.

The Group CEO has outlined her business goals of revenue, profit, accrual of customer data, and increased asset values to keep the shareholders happy. Originally, the Program would've simply had to secure the loyalty of the customers of its parent airline. But modern programs have extended their reach across all aspects of our daily spend.

The Program recruits other businesses to be part of the gig, let's call them **Partners**. These include travel suppliers, such as the Program's own parent airline, alliance and other partner airlines, hotel chains and accommodation wholesalers, and car hire, railway and cruise companies, and so forth.

They also include Partners offering cobranded credit cards and generic credit cards, plus tie-ins with financial suppliers covering insurance, mortgages, superannuation, foreign exchange, and investments.

The Program also recruits retail Partners. Some programs also set up an online mall to promote and centralize an online retail facility. Members can then conveniently purchase all sorts of goods online from hundreds of retailers through the one Internet portal, whilst earning points.

Now the Program can sell its points to its Partners to generate revenues potentially in the many billions of USDs (see Figure 6).

POINT BUSTER

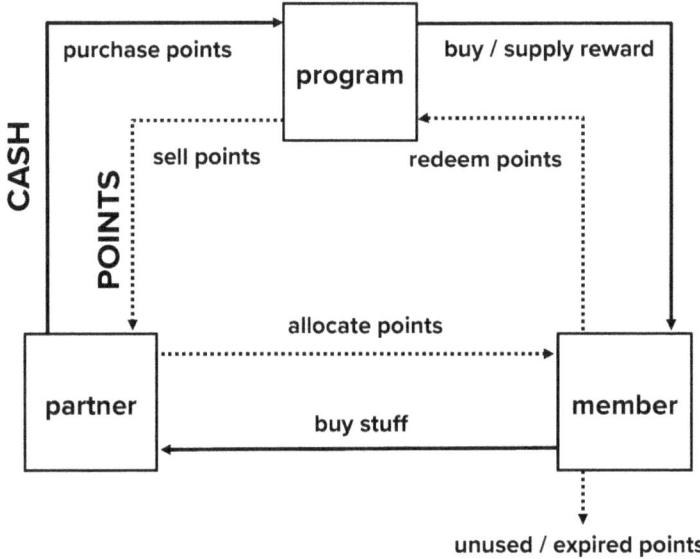

Figure 6: The circuit of cash and counterflow of points

According to the 2020 United Airlines *"MileagePlus Investor Presentation"*, that program generated USD5.3 billion through the sale of its miles in 2019. Delta Air Lines report *"Investor Day 2023"* cites annual revenue from its cobranded American Express card to be greater than USD6.5 billion.

The Program enlists everyday people in the tens of millions to sign up to join as **Members**, usually for free. United Airlines MileagePlus, Delta Air Lines SkyMiles, and American Airlines AAdvantage are widely reported to have over 100 million members each.

The Program also enrolls businesses as Members, with opportunities to earn points through Partners offering products tailored for travel and non-travel business needs. Discounts on airfares are offered per annual spend and points earned by a business can be transferred to employees.

For perspective, the *"Qantas Annual Report 2023"* claims that 450,000, or 19 percent of small and medium-sized business in Australia are members of the Qantas Business Rewards program.

Members buy stuff from the Partners and in return the Partners allocate Members the points, which the Partners bought from the Program. Huge amounts of cash can be spent within the money circuit of an airline loyalty program.

Members spent about USD50 billion when earning flyer points called Avios through everyday spending in 2019 according to the *"Capital Markets Day"* report from International Airlines Group (IAG), the parent company for airlines British Airways, Iberia, Aer Lingus, and Vueling.

The flow of cash from a Member to a Partner can also pass through the intermediate step of a credit card. Members can also earn points by spending cash with ***any*** business accepting the credit card, whether that business is a Partner or not.

IAG claims in their *"Capital Markets Day 2023"* report that holders of their cobranded credit cards spend over one percent of UK GDP, thereby, roughly USD30 billion, on their UK co-branded credit cards.

Delta Air Lines claim in their *"Investor Day 2023"* report that the spend by holders of the cobranded American Express cards is "approaching" one percent of US GDP, thereby trending towards roughly USD260 billion, if literally interpreted.

In both cases, the airline loyalty programs are taking their share of that spend by selling their points to the credit card companies, which, in turn, are using those points to encourage spend on their cards.

POINT BUSTER

There is a colossal retail and credit card cash flow, potentially worth hundreds of billions of USDs globally, and airline loyalty programs have a cut of all of that action.

Members have earned their points expecting rewards. The Program purchases those rewards from airlines and other suppliers and delivers them to Members, when they redeem their points. But not all Members redeem their points. Their points can expire under the rules set by the Program.

Now the Group CEO wants an update on financial performance, because it's business. Our Program can agree the sell price of points when they are purchased by the Partners **and** then set the effective buy-back price by balancing the cost to supply a given reward with the number of points required when Members redeem that reward.

The initial financial results for our hypothetical program are promising with the sell price of points to Partners set at USD15 cash per 1000 points. One third of that revenue is assigned to immediate costs, such as running and marketing the Program. Another third is allocated to purchase the reward.

That leaves a rather tidy gross profit of about 33 percent. For reference, according to the 2020 United Airlines *"MileagePlus Investor Presentation"*, the loyalty program earned 34 percent from its 2019 cash flow, whilst the *"Qantas Annual Report 2024"* claims an operating margin of 19.9 percent for that financial year for Qantas Frequent Flyer.

There is a delay from when points were sold to Partners until redeemed by Members. The Program can need to comply with accounting regulations and assign an amount to purchase the rewards later as a future liability in its accounts.

Now the Program can match the cost incurred when acquiring any given reward to the points that the member has to pony up to redeem that reward. Let's consider that the program has a target buy back price of USD5 per 1000 points.

Rewards include a limited number of plane seats, which the Program can access from the parent and partner airlines at some mutually agreed cost. If that cost to the Program is USD500, the seat can be made available to Members for 100,000 points, plus potentially a cash co-payment. The points required for other rewards can be pegged to their retail cost or are fully dynamic.

Finally, the Program is flexible. The points and cash co-payment needed for any given reward can be adjusted to balance profit, engagement of Members, legal compliance, liabilities on the books, and so forth. Winner, winner.

In short, we're not in an actual relationship with any given airline loyalty program. The loyalty universe is based upon sophisticated marketing models, expertly crafted to lock in our ongoing spend and scoop up our coin. Airline loyalty programs are just business.

Luckily, Pay-offs typically aren't fixed like the tenth coffee reward for loyal café spend. We can leverage the variation in Pay-offs to empower our cash spend for travel rich reward.

Basically, we can assess objectively what any given airline loyalty program has to offer. We can target wiser loyalty.

More Programs

We need to be flexible in our program selection to win the flyer point game. Being blindly loyal to just one program for so many years was the dumbest move that I ever made.

The airline concerned served me well and it all became very comfortable and familiar under my mistaken perception of shared loyalty, but I missed out on extraordinary opportunity by ignoring the benefits of playing the game across multiple airline loyalty programs.

By engaging with multiple programs, players can take advantage of their particular strengths and sweet spots and address the core challenge of limited reward seat availability.

Basically, we can harness the benefits of multiple programs. We don't need to be flying with the parent airline. We don't even need to be living in the same country where the parent airline is based. We can target more programs.

Better Fit

Our selection of airline loyalty programs impacts our gameplay. From the outside, programs appear to be broadly similar. They offer opportunities to earn their points and redeem rewards, and attain different levels of status offering varying potentially beneficial features, such as priority check in and access to an airline lounge.

But there are also differences. These include the availability of reward seats, the number of points required for rewards, the cash co-payments levied when we redeem our points for reward seats, the opportunities to earn our points, and access to reward seats of partner airlines, and so forth. Some programs release unsold seats close to the date of travel giving those players able to book late an advantage over those players who don't enjoy such flexibility in their travel plans.

GOALS

Players can decide which airline loyalty programs meet their goals, needs, and wants. They can even ask which is best. However, rather than assume that one program is better or worse than another, it makes sense to cherry pick their strengths.

Basically, we can broaden our engagement across multiple airline loyalty programs and thereby develop our strategy to take advantage of particular program attributes, that can help us to attain our own personal redemption goals. We can target better fit.

JUST LIVE IT: *play the programs*

(Hulopo'e Bay, Four Seasons Resort Lāna'i)

Success - Brisbane to Honolulu
Hawaiian Airlines Business Class
(American Airlines AAdvantage)

Rewards

Our goal for rewards is to redeem our points for a reward that can meet our needs and wants, whilst also unleashing great value from our flyer points.

Let's take a closer look at what lies within the fourth circle of the POINT BUSTER. The circle of REWARDS represents the rewards that we can redeem (see Figure 7).

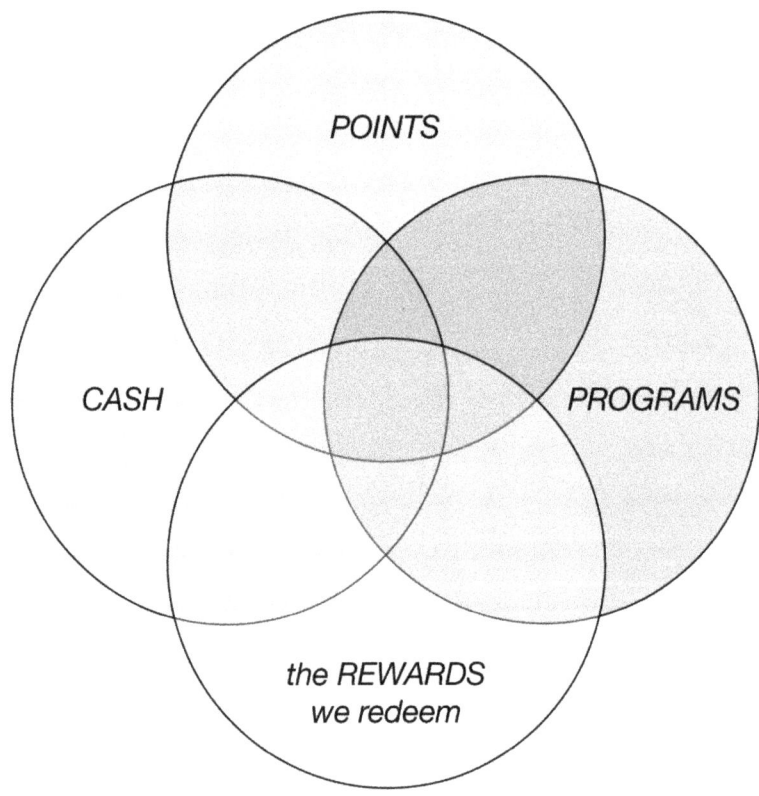

Figure 7: The REWARDS we redeem

Rewards include seats on a plane, hotel rooms, car hire, merchandise, gift vouchers, a luxury train ride, and even a charity donation, depending upon the airline loyalty program. The detail is typically available on the website of a given program's parent airline.

Imagine that customers of the local café pay for their first nine coffees and are rewarded with any number between one and ***dozens*** of coffees, not just the one. That paints a picture of what can happen in the flyer point game. Different players experience different reward for the same loyal spend.

Put another way, consider being rewarded with a credit voucher with any value between USD5 and USD9000 towards a future purchase when spending USD1000 on stuff in a shop. That illustrates the variation that I've experienced in the Qantas Frequent Flyer program to cite one example.

That stunning variation depends upon how easily we earn our points in the first place and the redeemed value delivered by those points when redeeming our reward.

To satisfy our rewards goal to redeem rewards that meet our needs and wants, whilst enjoying relatively better redeemed value for our flyer points, the POINT BUSTER targets richer reward, less cost, and greater access.

Richer Reward

We'll find that we can enjoy travel richer reward by selecting certain reward seats on a plane. For this book, I've classified rewards into three categories, which differ in the number of points required for a reward, the redeemed value that players can extract from their flyer points, and how easily that they can find a given reward (see Figure 8).

POINT BUSTER

	Award Seat	Dynamic Reward	Retail-based Reward
Pricing Basis	fixed cost	complex	retail cost
Redeemed Value	richer	variable	poorer
Points Required	less	variable	more
Availability	limited	variable	unlimited
Award Chart	yes	partial / none	none

Figure 8: Reward types

Award Seats are mostly for seats on a plane and include those for which the required number of points is correlated, in some way, to a cost of supply mutually agreed upon by the program and the airline.

The airline loyalty program has acquired some reward seats to offer for redemption at a cost price well below the retail airfare. The number of points required for such a reward is thereby calculated against that cost of supply, not the retail cost of the airfare.

Typically, the cost in points required for a given Award Seat is fixed. Thus, a one-way business class Saver Award to fly from Singapore to Istanbul using KrisFlyer miles on Singapore Airlines is currently set at 56,500 miles, if available.

Programs that offer such rewards typically have an online calculator or publish award charts on their parent airline's website. We can check the required number of points for a given airline, route, and cabin class. We know exactly where we stand and receive relatively good redeemed value for our flyer points.

Dynamic Rewards require varying numbers of points for a given reward. If we go to the parent airline's website and look for a reward seat for the same route over a range of dates, we'll see that the number of points needed is not fixed, but can be different on different days and flights. I checked a range of dates on the Delta Air Lines website. A one-way Delta One business class reward seat from New York to London required between 155,000 and 375,000 SkyMiles.

Dynamic pricing of rewards allows the airline loyalty program to be flexible. That pricing has been determined by various factors that might include the retail cost of the equivalent airfare.

Programs with such reward pricing may not publish an award chart or online calculator on their parent airline's website. Some do, but only with partial information, such as the minimum number of points or the range of points required for a given reward.

We have to do a test reward booking on the airline's website and then do the math to identify rewards offering relatively better redeemed value for our flyer points. In some cases, we can extract relatively good and in others very poor redeemed value.

I personally prefer to classify Dynamic Rewards further. There are some which very obviously require a number of points which track the equivalent retail piece of the reward. I've called them ***Retail-based Rewards*** in this book

These can include rewards for car hire, accommodation, corporate training, trips to the cinema, fuel, gift vouchers, and wine, even tickets to Broadway shows, depending upon the airline loyalty program itself.

If the retail cash cost for a camera is 20 times that of a toaster, then we can expect the reward redemption for that camera would require 20 times more points.

Some airline loyalty programs offer reward seats, which appear dynamic because the required number of points can differ for the same reward. But the redeemed value for our points is always very similar. Thus, I found that whereas the number of Qantas Frequent Flyer points varied for a *Classic Plus Reward Seat* in business class from Auckland to New York on Qantas Airways, their redeemed value was roughly the same at USD11 per 1000 points across different dates. The number of points was simply pegged to the retail price of the equivalent airfare.

Basically, we can learn how to identify the different types of reward and favor those that offer relatively higher redeemed value. We can target richer reward.

Less Cost

We can avoid having to redeem relatively huge numbers of points for the same reward seat. Would you rather redeem either 70,000 or 600,000 points for exactly the same seat, in the same cabin class, on the same flight?

We can come across somebody on a travel blog airing their frustration about the huge number of points required for their desired reward seats on a plane.

Searching for reward seats on some airlines' websites, we can see that they're absolutely right. There are business class international reward seats requiring hundreds of thousands of points and first-class flights for over a million points each way.

Luckily, there's an out. Those three types of reward are priced differently. They can require different numbers of points for the same route and cabin class. We simply need to learn how to tell them apart when searching for reward seats.

Let's go back to our **Retail-based Rewards**. We'll need relatively higher numbers of points for our reward. The redeemed value per batch of points is fairly fixed and similar within a given airline loyalty program. The catch is that such rewards offer relatively low redeemed values for our points.

Let's look at an example in which we can easily mix our points and cash when completing the online payment process. When searching for a one-way premium economy flight from Sydney to Johannesburg, the Qantas Airways website booking engine had a slider that let me reduce the retail airfare by spending points. It required 611,980 points and a co-payment of about USD170. The potential redeemed value was roughly USD3.10 for every 1000 points redeemed.

Now let's compare that to an **Award Seat**. By contrast such rewards typically require relatively lower numbers of points in order to redeem our reward. They sit at the higher end of redeemed values for our points.

In the scenario above, the premium economy seat was also available as an Award Seat, called a *Classic Flight Award* by Qantas Airways, requiring 71,100 points and a cash co-payment of about USD170. The potential redeemed value was about USD30 per 1000 points.

In this case, we'd have needed about 8.5 times less points to make a comparable redemption. That's about 8.5 times more redeemed value when selecting an Award Seat rather than the points-plus-pay Retail-based Reward.

Obviously, it's absolutely vital to be able to tell the difference between Dynamic Rewards, Retail-based Rewards, and Award Seats when searching online for our reward seat. We can be much better off by targeting Award Seats and Dynamic Rewards requiring significantly less points. These can offer relatively good redeemed value for our flyer points.

Award Seats are revealed when the number of points required for a reward seat matches that published in an award chart or online calculator on the parent airline's website. The number of points required to redeem any given itinerary is fixed. There can be different award charts for the program's parent airline and the partner airlines.

There are a number of variations in how Award Seats are actually priced in points by airline loyalty programs, which very basically relate to distance travelled and cabin class.

Some players like to use their points to upgrade from one cabin class to another, say from economy-coach to business class. The number of points for such an upgrade can also be published by the airline, so we can go and check how many points needed and request the upgrade on the airline website.

Finally, there are those **Dynamic Rewards**, which offer variable redeemed value. These can require relatively higher or lower numbers of points.

Thus, I found six different numbers of United Airlines MileagePlus miles required for a reward matching paid flights with exactly the same retail airfare, when searching for one-way business class direct Los Angeles to Sydney flights on United Airlines across a month of dates. The highest number of points was 2.5 times more than the lowest.

Basically, we can be faced with rewards requiring hugely variable numbers of points, reflecting reward seat pricing models. But we can favor those reward seats requiring relatively fewer points. We can target less cost.

Greater Access

To redeem relatively fewer points for a given reward and extract more redeemed value from our flyer points, we need to redeem our points for **Award Seats** and favorably priced **Dynamic Rewards**. Let's call them our **Target Rewards**.

The catch is that these tend to be in more limited supply. They have low availability because the airline of travel will only release a restricted number per flight, if any at all. In practice, they are much harder to find. Luckily, sometimes they can be available, but waiting to be found.

Seats on a given flight are perishable goods, like unsold fruit going rotten at a grocery store. If they are not sold or used, there is no second chance, that plane has flown. So, airlines apply yield management. They harness computer software programs to seek to maximize their revenue and minimize the empty seats on each flight. Airlines use many fare classes, which are defined by letters. Then they can allocate different airfares and sets of fare rules, even for seats on the same flight and in the same cabin class. Rewards seats are embedded in that system.

Basically, those reward seats offering relatively higher redeemed value are less available, but we can reveal those that are and simply waiting to be found. We can target greater access.

JUST LIVE IT: reap more reward

POINT BUSTER

(British Airways Concorde Room, Heathrow Airport)
LOSER TO WINNER

ACTIONS

It's time to learn proven actions that can satisfy our goals to target the most travel rich reward for our effort. We need to embrace four essential steps to play the flyer point game.

We **earn** points by spending cash, **match** our points to the program that meets our redemption goals, **search** out rewards from our programs of choice, and then **redeem** our reward. These fit neatly into the overlaps between two pairs of circles in the POINT BUSTER (see Figure 9).

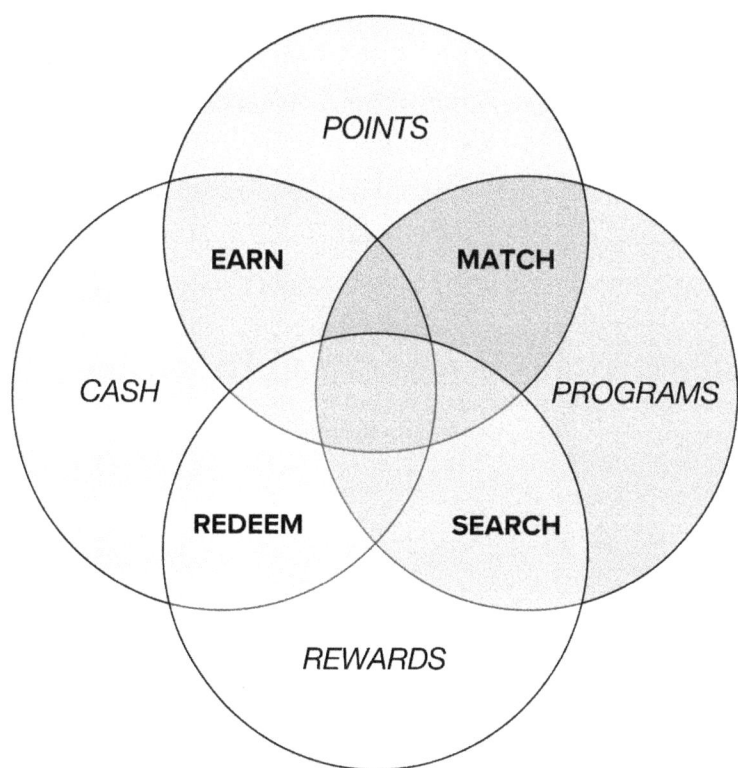

Figure 9: There are four essential steps

POINT BUSTER

Earn links our cash to our points. Match links our points to our programs. Search links our programs to our rewards. And redeem links our rewards back to our cash.

We're about to meet four power packs. **_PROPEL_** empowers a faster earn, **_SECURE_** empowers a stronger match, **_MASTER_** empowers a smarter search, and **_ENRICH_** empowers a wealthier redeem.

I've designed these power packs to bypass two fundamental speed bumps that will always keep some players in the slow lane.

On the one hand, our opportunity to be travel rich from everyday spend depends upon how efficiently we can unlock *value*. On the other hand, we have no control over the availability of differing types of rewards and that directly impacts our *odds of success*.

To add to the challenge, value and odds of success are intimately intertwined. Rewards offering relatively higher redeemed value tend to be less available and harder to find.

To complicate matters, players have different approaches to the concept of value, as discussed later in chapter VALUE. I've adopted objective measures in this book, because they're consistent and can be measured and applied by any player of the flyer point game. An objective approach opens a path for us to analyze our gameplay and then take control of our destiny in the flyer point game.

The POINT BUSTER can help to bypass those two speed bumps. Our four essential action steps can take us on the fast circuit to success, rather than leave us behind on a slower path.

ACTIONS

The actions within power packs PROPEL and ENRICH can steer us around the speed bump of value through a faster earn and wealthier redeem.

The actions within power packs SECURE and MASTER can steer us around the speed bump of limited availability of relatively more valuable rewards, and thereby improve our odds of successfully redeeming our Target Rewards, through a stronger match and smarter search.

But because all of the underlying parts are inter-related, eventually, a winning Pay-off will depend upon combining all four power packs to supercharge our points.

JUST LIVE IT: hack proven actions

(Giudecca Canal, Venice)

Success - Venice to Frankfurt
Lufthansa Business Class
(United MileagePlus)

POINT BUSTER

Earn

Our first action objective is to earn more points and to do that faster. A glaring hole in our skillset is revealed when a Three-toed Sloth could crawl to our dream travel destination quicker than we can by saving and redeeming flyer points, because our points accrue far too slowly. It's time to give our points some sizzle or place our bets on the sloth.

Driving a fast car can be fun. Apart from the rush, we can arrive at our destination quicker and go further in less time. Cue a simple equation. Divide distance by time to calculate speed. The basic math provides a universal measure of whether we're traveling like a Three-toed Sloth or burning rubber.

It's a similar deal in the airline loyalty game, only this time we're seeking to earn our points faster to empower our everyday spend. Our simple starting equation is the number of points that we earn divided by USD spent. We'll call that our **Earn Rate**. Incidentally, I've used USDs in this book just to be consistent. In practice, we can use any cash currency of choice.

Now we can compare the impact of different opportunities to earn points. Clearly, earning 20 points per USD pumps up a higher total number of points than earning 5 points per USD for the same cash spent, whatever the airline loyalty program.

Sometimes the math is easy because the supplier already quotes an offer in points per USD. At the American Airlines AAdvantage eShopping website, there's a wide range of Earn Rate, conveniently cited at from 1 to 25 miles or more per USD.

ACTIONS

Otherwise, the math is quite simple. Take the points earned and divide that by the dollars spent earning the points. Let's practice. I recently spent USD35 in a store and received 525 Qantas Frequent Flyer points. That works out to be 525 divided by 35, or 15 points per USD.

It's time to harness two basic tricks. Firstly, we can seek to increase the amount of our cash spend that earns points, and secondly, earn more points for each buck spent. Our power pack **PROPEL** has six practical actions designed to do just that and generate higher Earn Rates (see Figure 10).

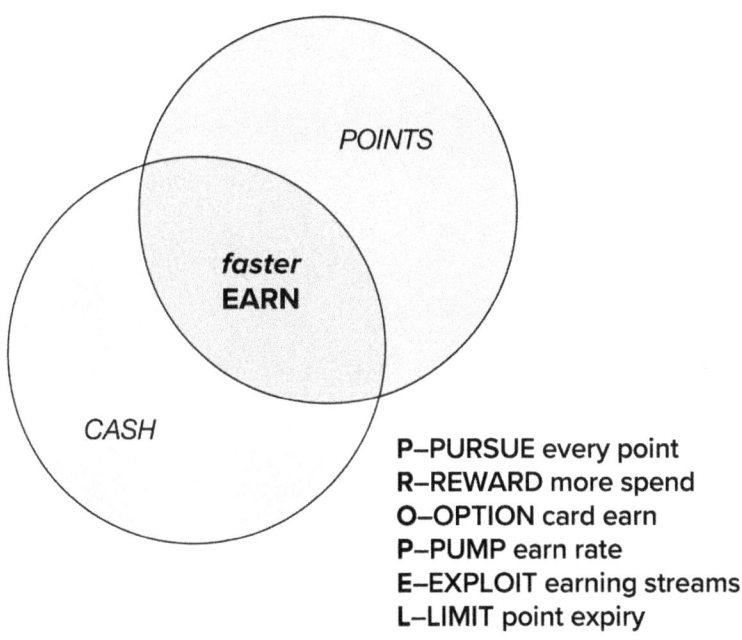

Figure 10: Six actions propel a faster earn

POINT BUSTER

Our points totals become accelerated because we simply multiply cash spend by Earn Rate to work out total points.

To appreciate the impact, let's compile a simple times table with our Earn Rate along the horizontal axis and our cash spend along the vertical axis. We can easily read off the total points accrued through any combination of cash spend and Earn Rate (see Figure 11).

		\	\	\	\	\	1000s points earned	\	\	\
CASH SPEND (1000s USD)	10	50	100	150	200	250	300	350	400	450	500
	9	45	90	135	180	225	270	315	360	405	450
	8	40	80	120	160	200	240	280	320	360	400
	7	35	70	105	140	175	210	245	280	315	350
	6	30	60	90	120	150	180	210	240	270	300
	5	25	50	75	100	125	150	175	200	225	250
	4	20	40	60	80	100	120	140	160	180	200
	3	15	30	45	60	75	90	105	120	135	150
	2	10	20	30	40	50	60	70	80	90	100
	1	5	10	15	20	25	30	35	40	45	50
		5	10	15	20	25	30	35	40	45	50
		EARN RATE (points per USD)									

Figure 11: Total points can be accelerated

Spending USD2000 at 10 points per USD can accrue 20,000 points. But if we can find opportunities to triple both to USD6000 at 30 points per USD, then we can accrue 180,000 points, some nine times more. There's a **_multiplier effect_** effectively helping us to save our points faster.

Let's run through the actions for a faster earn. But I can only put so much detail in one book, so I'll simply outline the core gambits, impacts, and attendant pitfalls. I'll also include how to kick start each action.

Pursue Every Point

Gambit: any transaction with the potential to earn flyer points is an opportunity for players to accrue more points. As a guiding principle, it's better to snatch up the points on offer rather than leave them behind.

Impact: pursuing every point increases our total points. Even small numbers of points earned over multiple transactions can add up. Earning, say, 2,000 points when shopping for weekly groceries alone tallies up to over 100,000 points in one year. We're missing out, by not grabbing those points.

Kick start: players enroll to become a member of one or more airline loyalty programs on the parent airlines' websites. Then they simply swipe their memberships cards at the till, or input their membership numbers, when buying online from a program's parent airline or its partner.

Players can log into a program's online shopping mall to receive points earned through its retail partners. They can also add their membership numbers to a travel booking.

Choice of program can be guided by how easy it is to earn points given where we live and our pattern of everyday spend. To get started, we can join one or more programs based in our own country, since it's likely there'll be readily accessible opportunity to earn points across many local program partners.

Location can be less relevant when we earn points for travel, given the opportunity to earn points across any number of airline loyalty programs for the same aircraft seat purchased.

Examples: I am a member of my local airline loyalty programs, Qantas Airways Frequent Flyer and Virgin Australia Velocity, since it's relatively easy to accrue and then restock redeemed points in those programs. Family in the USA likewise accrue points in one or more of the loyalty programs of the major US-based airlines.

Catch: other factors can affect our choice of program, such as sweet spots, reward seat availability, and the ability to transfer generic credit card points into our airline loyalty program account. We'll discuss these in due course.

Reward More Spend

Gambit: quite simply, the more that players can direct their everyday personal, household, and business spend through airline loyalty programs, the more points that they can accrue and more travel rich reward that they can enjoy.

Impact: all things being equal, if we can double that proportion of our spend, which earns flyer points, we can save our flyer points twice as fast.

Kick start: we can earn points buying airfares, other travel, groceries, wine, fuel, gift vouchers, electrical goods, setting up superannuation accounts, successfully applying for new credit cards, taking out a mortgage, and renewing our insurances for health, home, and vehicle, and so forth, depending upon the program and its partners.

ACTIONS

We can list items of personal, household, and business expenditure and then search out a matching point earning opportunity for each of our expense line items.

We can unearth the relevant point earning opportunities by checking out the program partners listed on the loyalty program pages of the airlines' websites and those of associated loyalty programs. We can also check out the online retail malls offered by some airline loyalty programs, which typically have hundreds of associated retail stores.

We can seek out the dedicated business programs, which are offered by some airline loyalty programs, to earn points through our business expenditure and transactions, such as travel, fuel, marketing and office supplies, paying tax and bills, exchanging currencies, processing EFTPOS sales, and so forth.

Examples: programs offering online malls include United's MileagePlus Shopping with over 1100, American Airlines AAdvantage eShopping with over 1200, and Delta Air Lines SkyMiles Shopping with over 1000 stores.

Associated loyalty programs, include the Nectar loyalty card in the UK, which encompasses over 500 partners, including the grocery chain, Sainsbury's. Nectar interlinks with the British Airways Club for collectors of their points, called Avios. Similarly, in Australia, the Everyday Rewards program aligns with Qantas Airways Qantas Frequent Flyer, and Flybuys with Virgin Australia Velocity.

The various business reward programs, include Emirates Business Rewards, Delta Air Lines SkyMiles for Business, and Virgin Australia Business Flyer, to cite just a few.

Catch: we have to be careful not to pay above the market rate just to get the points. The essential trick is to earn our points from the everyday cash that we'd be spending anyway.

Option Card Earn

Gambit: some credit cards are co-branded with the card issuer and a given airline loyalty program. Players then have the option to earn that program's flyer points whenever and wherever they pay for anything using the card.

Impact: cobranded cards extend our reach to earn points with any supplier, which accepts the card, not just the partners of a given airline loyalty program.

Cobranded cards can elevate the points earned through our everyday spend with Earn Rates typically in the range of one or less to 5 points per USD, depending upon where we live, the card product, and the items purchased.

Cards can also offer the incentive of a substantial points bonus once the card application has been approved. We typically need to spend a certain minimum amount in a defined timeframe. Accordingly, some players strategically churn their credit cards to milk the sign-up bonus offers, so amassing large numbers of points.

A sign-up bonus of 60,000 points with a minimum spend of USD3000 in 3 months, effectively delivers an Earn Rate of 20 points per USD, above the base Earn Rate within that honeymoon period. Some cards also offer bonuses, when we keep the card for a defined period.

Credit cards offer business owners with substantive cash flow an opportunity to amass large numbers of points through their ongoing business expenditure.

Some players carry multiple credit cards so that they can select the card for a given purchase, which offers the higher Earn Rate for the applicable purchase category, be that travel, or dining, and so forth.

Opportunities depend upon where we live, given differences in local financial regulations. Accordingly, there's greater scope for US-based and lesser scope for Australian or European based players.

Kick start: we can track down detailed information on co-branded credit cards to guide our choices through an online search citing the name of a chosen airline and the words "credit card".

Card products are frequently the subject of travel blog articles, since they offer a ready means to accrue points and some blogs attract revenue through their affiliations with card issuers, as duly disclosed on those blogs.

Examples: co-branded credit cards are available encompassing a wide range of the major airline loyalty programs. These include the Aegean Bonus Visa, the Virgin Atlantic Reward+, and the avianca life**miles** American Express Elite cards, to name just a few.

Catch: the credit card issuer can levy an annual fee, which can be in the hundreds of dollars, although we can decide to balance that cost against card features, such as earning airline status, companion award certificates, and fee waivers when changing or refunding award tickets, if of value to us personally.

A co-branded card locks us into the one airline loyalty program, unlike generic cards, which we'll discuss later.

Credit cards can attract relatively high interest rates on carried forward unpaid balances. It's outside of the scope of this book to recommend such products or provide financial advice.

Pump Earn Rates

Gambit: players can seek out ways to earn more points for each dollar spent. Fortunately, certain transactions can offer relatively higher Earn Rates and / or some bonus points.

Impact: accrual of flyer points can be greatly increased. I recently earned about 30 points per USD through some grocery shopping and about 300 points per USD during a telco's SIM card promotion, respectively over 30 and 300 times higher than the typical base Earn Rate for the associated program. Obviously, opportunities to do so depend upon the program and available bonus point offers.

Kick start: we can sign up for promotional emails through our online accounts for a given airline loyalty program and its associated partners and programs.

We can check airline websites and online shopping malls for bonus point offers and scan the headlines of our preferred travel blogs for relevant news on promotional offers. We can also keep an eye out for bonus points offered for the purchase of gift vouchers.

Examples: at the AAdvantage eShopping mall the bonus offers are always changing, but there are typically Earn Rates in the ballpark of 5 to 25 miles per USD. I was recently able to buy Apple Gift Vouchers from my local grocery store with a bonus of about 30 points per USD.

Catch: finding such opportunities can require effort. Once again, we need to be careful not to pay above the market rate just to get the points.

Exploit Earning Streams

Gambit: sometimes players can earn more points by stacking multiple point earning opportunities for the same transaction.

Impact: players can accumulate points many times faster than a typical base rate. Firstly, they can pay for a point earning transaction by using a point earning cobranded card for a two-stream stack. These add together, so a base Earn Rate of 1 point per USD when buying stuff paid with a card earning 3 points per USD stacks to 4 points per USD.

One option is to seek bonus offers on airline loyalty program online malls. Players can stack up another stream when they make that purchase during a promotional offer of bonus point earn, say, of 5 points per USD. Now they add all three to enjoy a total Earn Rate of 9 points per USD.

Sometimes, players can add a fourth stream of earning points when there are bonuses to encourage spend through the online mall. Thus, a bonus of 3000 points for a minimum USD1000 spend would step up the Earn Rate by up to another 3 points per USD.

If players make the purchase as part of reaching a minimum spend for a credit card sign-up bonus, they create a fifth stream of earning points. Using our earlier example, that's another 20 points per USD. The total Earn Rate has jumped up to 32 points per USD by stacking the earning streams.

Kick start: we can research such opportunities by checking airline websites for promotional offers, signing up for their marketing emails, and scanning the headlines of travel blogs for news of periodic deals.

Examples: I enjoyed an eight-way stack to pump up the Earn Rate purchasing Qantas Wine. The full stack propelled the Earn Rate from about 2 to about 100 points per USD.

Catch: as always, we need to avoid paying over the market rate for the goods and services purchased when earning points. Finding such opportunities requires some effort.

Limit Point Expiry

Gambit: points can expire in some airline loyalty programs. There are some things that players can do to keep their points and not lose them.

Impact: if our points expire, we forego any rewards, which we could have redeemed with those points.

Kick start: obviously, it makes sense to be familiar with the expiry rules for those programs to which we belong. We can keep a record of when our points are due to expire and what actions are needed to take to protect them.

Programs broadly adopt one of three approaches. Firstly, the points of some programs never expire, including the miles of United Airlines MileagePlus. Then there's nothing to worry about.

Secondly, some flyer points have a limited lifespan, but that can be reset with at least one qualifying activity within a past timeframe. Thus, avianca life**miles** has a 12-month and American Airlines AAdvantage an 18-month timeframe.

Luckily, point lifespans can be reset quite easily, typically by simply earning or redeeming some points, or other account activity. We need to check which activities count on the parent airlines' websites. For example, Etihad Guest miles can be extended beyond 18 months by taking a flight on the airline or its partners.

Thirdly, some programs' points expire after a defined lifespan regardless of account activity. Thus, Thai Airways Royal Orchid miles expire on a quarterly basis 36 months from accrual. However, some programs include options to extend point lifespans. Thus, Emirates Skywards miles don't expire if members hold a Skywards cobranded credit card or achieve the Skywards Platinum status tier.

Examples: Singapore Airlines KrisFlyer miles have to be redeemed within 36 months since their month of accrual, but members can pay a fee to defer expiry for 6 months, or 12 months, if they hold Silver or Gold Elite status.

Members can double check whether their miles are due to expire on their online accounts. The airline periodically sends emails to its members showing whether miles are due to expire.

Catch: it can be harder to accrue the total points that we need for our goal redemption in those programs with a fixed-point lifespan. We may need to transfer points from a generic credit card or other allied account to reach our target before our points start to expire.

JUST LIVE IT: propel a faster earn

POINT BUSTER

(United Airlines Boeing B787 Dreamliner over the Pacific Ocean)

ROOKIE TO CHAMP

Match

Our second action objective is to match our points to our travel goals, basically, to group and allocate them across programs now, so that there are more search options when the time comes later to redeem them for our desired reward.

Imagine obediently waiting to open a beautifully wrapped present until our actual birthday, only to find there's sweet nothing at all inside, because somebody thought that the fun of sending us on an emotional ride with zero reward was worth the cost of the wrapping, but not an actual gift.

Yes, many of us have been there, the second glaring hole in our skillset is revealed, when we can't find our goal rewards.

Let's define ***Options,*** a measure of how well our points portfolio matches our redemption goal. It's simply the number of reward search options that we expect to have, when the time comes to redeem our flyer points.

Imagine lining up extra unopened presents, in case we need to unwrap multiple presents to find the gift that we actually need or want.

There are two tricks. One is to decide to which loyalty accounts to allocate our points. The other is to batch given numbers of points to a chosen account to match how many points are required to redeem for our goal reward.

Our power pack **SECURE** has six practical actions designed to do just that and generate more search Options (see Figure 12).

POINT BUSTER

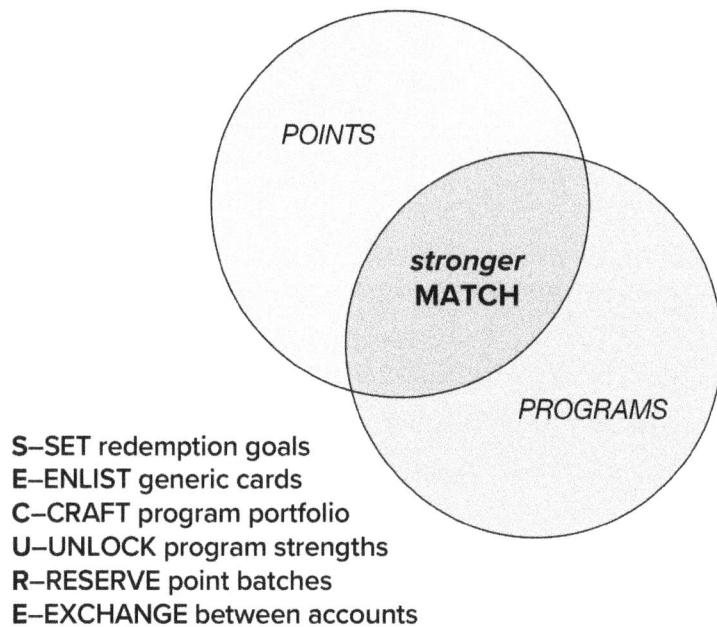

S–SET redemption goals
E–ENLIST generic cards
C–CRAFT program portfolio
U–UNLOCK program strengths
R–RESERVE point batches
E–EXCHANGE between accounts

Figure 12: Six actions secure a stronger match

Obviously, the actual number of points required for a given reward redemption will depend upon the program and the reward.

The number of search Options will depend upon our selection of itinerary and airline loyalty programs, and how we assign our points totals between those programs

Let's consider the impact. When searching for reward seats on one date on daily flight on one airline on a direct route, there is only one search Option. But when searching across three airlines each with two flights per day over each day within a five-day period, our Options have escalated to 30. Adding two alternative and similarly served departure and arrival airports then drives the number of Options up to 120.

ACTIONS

(Kurilpa Bridge, Brisbane)
EXPERIENCE CITIES

We can jiggle the numbers to suit our situation, but the basic math still applies. There's another ***multiplier effect***, this time driving power pack SECURE. We want our match and batch actions to unlock that very flexibility (see Figure 13).

ELEMENT	OPTIONS PER ELEMENT	CUMULATIVE TOTAL OPTIONS
Direct routes	1	1
Flights per day	2	2
Airlines	3	6
Days	5	30
Departure airports	2	60
Arrival airports	2	120

Figure 13: Total search Options can be accelerated

Let's run through the actions for a stronger match. But I can only put so much detail in one book, so I'll simply outline the core gambits, impacts, and attendant pitfalls. I'll also include how to kick start each action.

Set Redemption Goals

Gambit: players can set their redemption goals, how they'd like to harness their points to address their own personal travel needs and wants at some time in the future.

Impact: without a plan we're playing the flyer point game blind. At best we risk simply letting our points accrue until there's just enough to redeem for an immediate need or want. At worst, we risk never making a redemption and letting our flyer points expire unused.

Alternatively, specific redemption goals can determine how we manage our portfolio of points, how to accrue and allocate our points across one or more of our selected airline loyalty accounts, and then which rewards that we can redeem.

Kick start: we can compile an ideal travel itinerary based upon our future travel plans. We can then research what airlines have relevant scheduled flights to identify potential search Options for reward seats, which can satisfy our goals.

Examples: I have a redemption goal of flying between Colombia and Spain to visit family. Checking on Google Flights, that's possible on the direct flights of Avianca, or Iberia, or Air Europa. Now I can manage my points to be able to access any available rewards on those airlines.

Catch: our goals need to be adaptable, since programs can shift the goal posts and airlines continually adjust their schedules and reward seat availability.

Being flexible in our redemption goals can add Options. If it's hard to redeem points for our first-choice date or destination, we may still be able to redeem for alternatives.

Enlist Generic Cards

Gambit: some credit cards are cobranded and locked into the one airline loyalty program, but others are generic. Players can accrue card points and then transfer them to a range of airline loyalty programs just when needed, thereby harnessing great flexibility.

Impact: like cobranded cards, generic cards can offer a sign-up bonus, typically with a minimum spend in a time period, offering a route to a swag of flyer points at a relatively high Earn Rate.

Being able to transfer card points to multiple airline loyalty program accounts just when we find our desired rewards, generates timely and extraordinary flexibility.

That can be potentially game changing, especially for those players, who are able to accumulate substantial credit card point totals.

Kick start: we can do online searches to research the details of various generic credit cards. Generic cards are frequently discussed on travel blogs.

To transfer card points we go to our card's online account, surf to partner transfers, and enter the details of the transfer, including the airline loyalty program and number of card points to transfer. We can enter our airline loyalty program details into our card online account in advance.

There can be periodic transfers bonuses. Friend, David, transferred his Canadian-based American Express Platinum card points to British Airways Club Avios during a 40 percent bonus offer.

Examples: my Australian-based American Express Platinum Card offers the option to transfer to 13 airline loyalty programs. I can also transfer to the hotel loyalty program, Marriott Bonvoy, and then from there to about 40 airline loyalty programs.

Catch: our card points need to be transferred to an airline loyalty program before they can be redeemed for a reward. We can't transfer the points back again.

A transfer bonus may or may not coincide with an opportunity to transfer card points for a given reward opportunity.

Card points can transfer almost immediately or it can take one or more days. We can check typical transfer times through our card online accounts and reports on travel blogs.

Credit cards are a financial product offering credit typically at relatively high interest rates on unpaid balances. It's outside the scope of this book to recommend any such products or provide financial advice.

Craft Program Portfolio

Gambit: players can generate exponentially escalating search Options for reward seats when it comes to redeem their points by engaging in more than one airline loyalty program.

Impact: sometimes the one airline loyalty program quite simply doesn't offer the reward seat availability to meet our redemption goal. Then we have to change our plans or miss out entirely. We can lower the risk of that happening by diversifying our engagement across multiple programs and thereby generating more reward seat search Options.

Kick start: the obvious way to diversify is to be active in at least one of the airline loyalty programs from each major alliance, **one**world, Star Alliance and SkyTeam, to access reward seats across their allied airlines.

There are also some airlines sitting outside the three major airline alliances to consider. By way of example, we can currently access reward seats on Qatar Airways through Virgin Australia Velocity.

When carrying a generic credit card, we can sign up to those airline loyalty programs to which we can transfer our generic credit card points.

Examples: I depend upon the flexibility of multiple airline loyalty programs to satisfy my travel goal of complex round-the-world itineraries in business and first class.

One recent trip included redemptions using Alaska Airlines Mileage Plan miles for Qantas Airways business class, avianca life**miles** for Lufthansa business class, Qantas Frequent Flyer points for British Airways first class, and Virgin Australia Velocity for Singapore Airlines business class.

Catch: not all reward seats are available when redeeming our points of one airline loyalty program for reward seats on an allied airline.

We can choose to favor those programs, which appear to release reward seats preferentially to their own members. These include Qantas Frequent Flyer, Singapore Airlines KrisFlyer, and Etihad Guest, to name just a few.

We also need to decide how much diversity is a good thing. Insufficient diversity can reduce access to available reward seats and to individual program strengths. Excessive diversity can dilute the total number of points in each of the accounts in our portfolio, so leaving us short for the total points needed to redeem for our redemption goal.

Unlock Program Strengths

Gambit: airline loyalty programs can look similar, but have different strengths and sweet spots. Players can match these to their travel goals.

Impact: choice of airline loyalty program can affect how easily we earn our points, how much redeemed value that we can extract for our points, and our access to reward seats meeting our redemption goals.

Kick start: we can research specific program's strengths and sweet spots online. These are often discussed on travel blogs.

We also need to factor in typical patterns of reward availability. Test bookings on the airlines' websites can reveal the typical availability of our goal reward. We can research travel blog articles reporting releases of reward seats and whether a given airline typically releases unsold seats as reward seats close to the date of departure.

Now that the frequent spender is part of the flyer point game, it also makes sense to consider programs offering relatively broader opportunities to earn our points, as well as relatively better scope to secure higher Earn Rates or Returns to empower our Pay-off.

Examples: I usually have a stash of British Airways Club Avios to redeem for the sweet spot of relatively short distance flights in business class, such as flights on British Airways or Iberia within Europe or travel between Australian city pairs on partner airline Qantas Airways.

Some rewards offer differing combinations of numbers of Avios and cash co-payments. I can thereby redeem small numbers of Avios for long distance business class reward seats by upping the cash component of the reward, whilst still unlocking relatively high redeemed value for my Avios.

Catch: we have to plan ahead and assess the fitness of our program selections as part of a forward strategic plan. In that time, programs can change and increase the points needed for our goal redemption.

Reserve Point Batches

Gambit: rather than focus on total points, players can seek to batch that total up to match the numbers of points needed for their redemption goals.

Impact: batching points is a way of planning and an essential tool for a systematic approach to aligning our points with our travel goals.

Kick start: we can check the number of points needed for our goal redemption on the websites of those airlines, which offer award charts and online calculators. For programs without award charts, test reward bookings on the parent airline website can reveal the lowest number of points needed for our chosen route and cabin class.

We can aim to save up and then have batches of points ready to redeem or transfer in one or more program accounts and program partner accounts.

Examples: to travel first class return between Doha and Istanbul on Qatar Airways currently we'd need two batches of 61,000 Virgin Australia Velocity points, totaling 122,000.

Catch: in the time it takes us to save and batch up our points, the relevant airline loyalty program can have moved the goal posts by increasing the number of points needed for our desired redemption.

Programs with dynamic pricing present a huge variation in points needed for the same flight sector in the same class, making it difficult to plan for our redemption goal.

Exchange Between Accounts

Gambit: players generally have to commit to one airline loyalty program account when they earn their flyer points. But in some situations, they can exchange their points between accounts.

Impact: transferring points can extend our opportunities to earn and group points and to harness any periodic transfer bonuses. Transfers can also offer a handy way of topping up points, when just short of points for our goal redemption. Sometimes we can group points from more than one member, so increasing the total number of accessible points.

Kick start: it's prudent to research online which points can be transferred into and out of our airline loyalty programs of choice as well as the detail on the actual process.

Examples: program members can transfer flyer points called Avios between the British Airways Club and Aer Lingus AerClub, Iberia Plus, Qatar Airways Privilege Club, and Finnair Plus.

Members can transfer either way between Singapore Airlines KrisFlyer miles and Virgin Australia Velocity points, albeit at a losing conversion rate of receiving one for 1.55 points or miles.

Members can make transfers of points between family members within Virgin Australia Velocity and Qantas Frequent Flyer.

Household accounts with the facility to pool total points of family members are offered by the British Airways Club, Qatar Airways Privilege Club, avianca life**miles**, and of family and friends by Virgin Atlantic Flying Club. Scandinavian Airlines EuroBonus offers the facility for a point sharing group across between two and eight members.

In other programs, such as United Airlines MileagePlus and avianca life**miles**, members can transfer points between members for a fee.

POINT BUSTER

Sometimes we can transfer points saved through a third-party loyalty program into an airline loyalty program. Thus, various reward programs points can be converted to Singapore Airlines KrisFlyer miles.

Some hotel chain loyalty program points can be transferred to airline loyalty programs. Thus, World of Hyatt members can transfer points to about 25 and Accor Live Limitless to about 30 airline loyalty programs.

Catch: we can typically enjoy more redeemed value through the original loyalty program in which we earned our points. But making the transfer during a bonus offer can shift the math. It's wise to run the numbers before committing to a transfer.

JUST LIVE IT: secure a stronger match

(Regent Street, London)

Success - Tokyo to London
British Airways First Class
(American Airlines AAdvantage)

Search

If players can't find or book their reward seats of choice, they can end up stuck where they are, and not going anywhere fast. Our third action objective is to increase the probability of finding the reward that we seek through a smarter search.

We can't change limited reward seat availability, but we can still take the time and effort to improve our ability to find those reward seats that are waiting to be found.

Our power pack ***MASTER*** has six practical actions designed to elevate the probability of finding our goal rewards (see Figure 14).

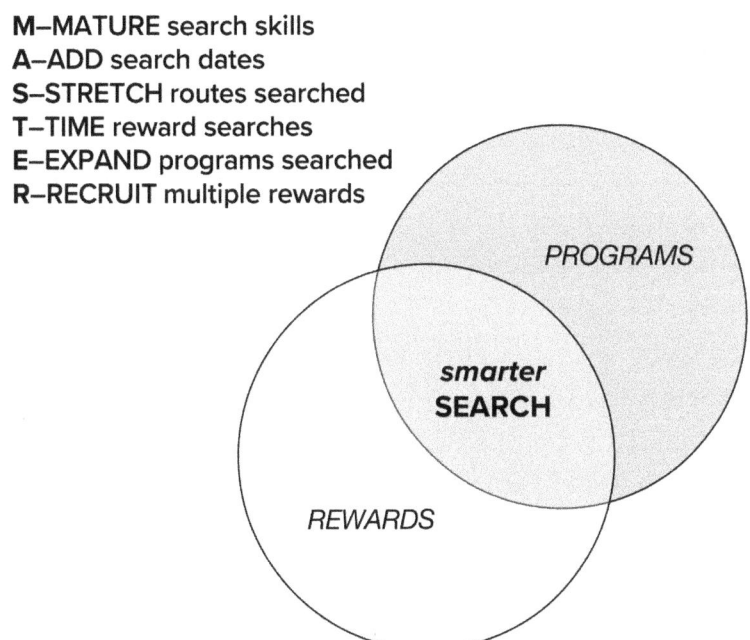

Figure 14: Six actions master a smarter search

Several challenges impact the likelihood of finding the rewards that we want. Firstly, our Target Rewards, namely, Award Seats and Dynamic Rewards offering relatively higher redeemed values, have to be released by the parent and their allied partner airlines. That's out of our control.

Secondly, there has to be sufficient flexibility in our program portfolio for us to be able to access those Target Rewards, which do become available. We've addressed that in chapter MATCH.

Thirdly, we can develop our search skills. Basically, if a Target Reward is available, we want to elevate the likelihood of finding it and doing so before any other players.

Given the challenges impacting our access to Target Rewards, we can define our **Chances**, a measure of the likelihood of successfully finding at least one Target Reward on any given flight search Option.

We don't know the likelihood of finding any given reward seat sometime in the future. But we can derive a **best estimate** by checking the availability of our Target Rewards over a number of future dates and flights. Thus, if we find at least one Target Reward in business class for about one tenth of the flights searched, then our best estimate of the Chances is 10 percent or 0.10.

Obviously, the actual likelihoods aren't constant, so we're just getting a feel for the overall pattern of Target Reward availability to guide our gameplay.

The impact of improving our reward search skills is considerable. We're potentially in competition for the same Target Rewards with millions of other players belonging to the same and allied airline loyalty programs.

Imagine that four reward seats are available waiting to be found. One player can only locate two of them. Another can find all four. Obviously, the skills of the second player bestow them with a significant advantage.

Let's run through the actions for a smarter search. But I can only put so much detail in one book, so I'll simply outline the core gambits, impacts, and attendant pitfalls. I'll also include how to kick start each action.

Mature Search Skills

Gambit: players can increase their Chances of revealing any available award seats by improving their intrinsic search skills to outwit the quirks and harness the strengths of the various airlines' websites.

Impact: even a small increase in our competency can greatly increase our Chances and give us the edge when searching for the same goal rewards as players with lesser skills.

Third-party online tools are also available, which automate the search, potentially saving much time and effort. These include Award Nexus, ExpertFlyer, and seats.aero, to name just a few without favor.

Kick start: we can search online for detailed advice on how to redeem our points on any particular airline's website. Travel blog articles sometimes offer such information.

We can also search out reward seats released by one airline on the website of one of its airline partners, to harness superior functions, such as a monthly calendar of reward availability.

We can do an online search for comparative reviews of the relative strengths of online search tools, thus whether they offer automated alerts and how often they refresh their data.

Examples: I couldn't book a one-way business class reward seat from Cairns to Los Angeles through the Qantas Airways website for a sample travel date. It showed no availability.

But I still found reward seats, by chunking the itinerary down into a search over each of two sectors via Sydney and then marrying them together using the multi-city function.

Catch: looking on one airline's website for reward seat availability released by another airline can be misleading, if the reward seat inventory hasn't been shared between programs.

Reward seats can appear when none in fact exists, so-called "ghost" availability. If unsure, we can cross check across more than one website or ring the airlines' call centers.

We have to be very careful to identify "mixed cabin" itineraries. Booking interfaces can display a premium reward comprising multiple flights when our chosen cabin class isn't available on one or more of the flight sectors.

Third-party online search tools generally require a paid subscription and vary in capability, for example, whether they can search a given airline, or over a range of dates or airports, or set up an alert.

We don't know how well the automated search is working without cross checking the results manually.

Add Search Dates

Gambit: sometimes players have a limited window of dates on which they can travel. But any flexibility in travel dates can broaden their search for reward seats.

ACTIONS

Impact: additional travel dates can have a multiplier effect on our search Options. If there are two flights per day and we can widen our search over five days we now have ten rather than just two search Options. Players with flexible travel plans have a potentially huge strategic advantage.

Kick start: it pays to think flexibly when planning any travel on reward seat redemptions. A relaxed and adaptable approach can mean being prepared to recast an itinerary, whilst still meeting our core travel goals.

Examples: I needed to travel from Australia to Spain to attend a wedding on a set date as part of a 3-week vacation. But the outbound and travel inbound dates still had some flexibility, since I could move the vacation days to suit the availability of reward seats.

Catch: those players who are locked into set or popular travel dates, such as school vacations, can find it harder to squeeze any flexibility in travel dates out of their schedule.

Stretch Routes Searched

Gambit: sometimes there's only one way to get from origin to destination. Otherwise, players can create a goal itinerary from any number and combinations of flights.

Impact: additional flexibility in our approach can increase our flight search Options exponentially and thereby greatly increase our Chances of finding the reward seats that we seek.

Kick start: we can research route combinations on airline websites and free third-party services, such as Google Flights.

POINT BUSTER

We can select a one-way option and enter our origin and destination and pick a date to get started. We can restrict the search to non-stop flights and then step up to select the one-stop or fewer selection, and so forth.

This book doesn't advocate any commercial products, but we can use website FlightConnections for some basic searches for free.

Armed with routing information, we can then search each component flight sector of our itinerary individually for reward seats on the website of the parent airline of the relevant airline loyalty program.

In practice, there can be less reward availability on some sectors than others, for example, on the longer transcontinental or transoceanic flights. It makes sense to focus our attention first on those sectors which offer the greater challenge in finding reward seat availability and then build a reward itinerary around them sector by sector.

Examples: I can't get to London from Cairns on one flight. There are several two-sector routings, namely, routing through Singapore, Tokyo, and seasonally, Hong Kong. Adding sectors grows routing combinations exponentially. There are dozens of three-sector routings.

Catch: adding a separate positioning flight or extra sector to complete an itinerary can incur an opportunity cost of paying more points, or the cash for the extra airfare and the accommodation costs of the stopover.

Time Reward Searches

Gambit: players can get ahead of the pack and give themselves their best chance of snaring the rewards that they seek by timing their search for reward seats to coincide with when they are typically released.

Impact: it's easy to forget that we're in competition for a limited resource with other players of the flyer point game. Those in the know plan and time their redemptions, so improving their odds of finding them before another player.

Kick start: airlines typically release their seats 11 to 12 months before the date of departure, although the exact number of days varies between airlines. We can aim to book our redemption as soon as the flights are released into the schedule. We can do an online search to find exactly how many days in advance a given airline will release its inventory.

Reward seats can crop up at any time as airlines jiggle their inventory. Release of reward seats can also occur in a batch. This can also happen when a new flight route is loaded into the system.

New routes and batch release of reward seats are sometimes covered in travel blogs, so a regular cursory scan of our favorite travel blogs can alert us to such availability.

We can always explore reward seat inventory by making test bookings on the various airlines' websites whenever needed.

It can be much easier to put together reward itineraries close to the date of travel, since some airlines make unsold inventory available for reward redemption.

Examples: I've booked Singapore Airlines First Class Suites from Singapore to London within a couple of minutes of their first release 355 days in advance.

By contrast, I've made many successful redemptions onto airlines that release reward seats close to the date of travel, including on Emirates and British Airways from one day to a couple of weeks before departure.

Catch: the same reward inventory can become available in one program before another, so members of the first program can access reward seats before members of the second, thus endowing a competitive advantage.

The further into the future that we redeem our reward seat, the more likely that there will be some change in schedule or aircraft type. We can choose an aircraft to enjoy a lie-flat business class seat, only to find an equipment change leads to a downgrade in cabin class or leaves us stuck with an inferior product. On the other hand, constructing reward seat itineraries close to the dates of travel requires last minute flexibility.

Expand Programs Searched

Gambit: players can check the availability of reward seats through more than one airline loyalty program to escalate their search Options across multiple airlines and routings.

Impact: searching across multiple airline loyalty programs can generate excellent flexibility and potentially access reward inventory from dozens of airlines, depending upon reward availability.

ACTIONS

Kick start: we can sign up to be a member of multiple airline loyalty programs, whether we regularly fly on, or live in the same country as the parent airline or not.

Our individual selection of airline loyalty programs depends upon our personal circumstances and travel goals, but it can make sense to diversify and become a member of at least one airline loyalty program from each of the major alliances. It can also be prudent to be a member of each of the programs to which we can transfer our generic credit card points.

Examples: my Qantas Frequent Flyer memberships allows me to access reward seats on Qantas Airways, but also opens options offered by other airlines from the **one**world Alliance and also about another 10 partner airlines, including Emirates, to total about 25 airlines.

Through Virgin Australia Velocity, I can access reward seats released by Virgin Australia and potentially access others on about 16 allied airlines.

My United Airlines MileagePlus membership also opens up the door to redeem my points on the other about 25 airlines from the Star Alliance to which United Airlines belongs, in addition to other partner airlines.

I can also engage though my American Express Platinum Card with Virgin Atlantic, which recently joined the global airline alliance, SkyTeam, which has about 19 airline members, adding about another 16 airlines, allowing for duplication between program partners.

Catch: players can't always rely on securing reward seats available on a given airline through a partner program. This is because reward seat inventory isn't always fully shared.

97

By way of example, I engage with Singapore Airlines KrisFlyer, so that I can access Award Seats issued by Singapore Airlines, which typically, but not always, appears to release more reward seats in business class and solely first / suites on Singapore Airlines itself to its own members.

Recruit Multiple Rewards

Gambit: players can start by searching for reward seats for their goal itinerary on the one redemption, but given the limited availability of more valuable rewards, that may not work. But they can chunk the itinerary into two or more bookings.

Impact: searching one component sector at a time across multiple programs can greatly increase our Chances of finding our desired reward seats.

Kick start: we can chunk our goal reward itinerary down into sectors and search for reward seat availability for each sector on the program's parent airline's website across multiple programs.

We can also snare what is available right now and then build the itinerary thereafter. Since cancelling or changing a booking can be free or incur only a small charge, depending upon the program, we can refine our travel plans later given changing reward seat inventory at low cost.

Examples: my recent round-the-world itinerary featured four redemptions, two using Qantas Frequent Flyer points, one using Singapore Airlines KrisFlyer miles and one using Alaska Airlines Mileage Plan miles. It started with just the Singapore to London sector. I added the other flights later.

ACTIONS

Catch: the more that we break down our journey into separate redemption bookings, the more time and energy is needed to construct and refine our bookings.

Multiple redemption bookings can also increase the number of points needed for the overall itinerary.

We need to be mindful of connection times, when spreading an arriving and departing flight over two separate bookings, and allow for a realistic buffer of time to make our connecting flight.

JUST LIVE IT: master a smarter search

(Iberia Express Airbus A321neo, Tenerife North Airport)

Success - Tenerife to Madrid
Iberia Business Class
(The British Airways Club)

Redeem

Our fourth action objective is to unlock more value from our points. Players can target a wealthier redeem by choosing those rewards that deliver relatively greater redeemed value. They can also favor reward seats offering an enhanced travel experience, such as those in premium cabin classes.

Players can be blind to a ten-times or more variation in redeemed value in the flyer point game. Imagine traveling and having to pay for stuff with an unfamiliar foreign currency and wondering why the bar staff are smiling in amazement, only to realize back at your hotel that you were tipping each Fuzzy Navel cocktail with a fifty-dollar note instead of a five-dollar bill.

The fourth glaring hole in our skillset is revealed when we're clueless about the redeemed value of our points and risk spending them frivolously.

To be winners, we need to embrace the reality that the redeemed value of our points is highly variable and only realized when we actually exchange our flyer points for a reward. This holds true when comparing similar redemptions between airline loyalty programs and different redemptions within the same program.

To measure the unlocked value of our points, we simply divide the redeemed value of the reward by the points required for that reward. Although some adopt cents per point, I adjust the result to be quoted in USD redeemed value per 1000 points, which will make our life much easier later on. We'll call this measure our ***Returns***.

ACTIONS

Let's practice with the example of redeeming 25,000 points for a gift voucher worth USD100. We simply divide the retail value by the number of 1000s of points, thus 100 divide 25, arriving at USD4 per 1000.

To determine redeemed value for a reward seat, we can check the equivalent retail airfare by making a test paid booking on the airline's website for the very same flight and cabin class as the reward seat.

There are a few challenges when calculating redeemed value for some reward seat redemptions, but there are easy solutions to arrive at a consistently applied measure.

Firstly, almost all Award Seats require a co-payment in cash as well as the points. In some cases, the cash co-payment is very small and won't unduly upset the math. But in other cases, the co-payment is significant and it makes sense to adjust our calculation accordingly.

The trick is to subtract the co-payment needed for the redemption from the retail value of the equivalent airfare to arrive at a more accurate estimate of redeemed value.

Let's try that. Imagine redeeming 20,000 points for a one-way economy-coach Award Seat. The retail airfare is USD400. Our rough estimate of Returns is 400 divided by 20, or USD20 redeemed value per 1000 points.

However, there is also a co-payment of USD100. So, let's adjust the redeemed value of the redemption, simply 400 minus 100, or USD300. Our more accurate estimate of Returns is now 300 divided by 20, or USD15 redeemed value per 1000 points. Whether we decide to make the adjustment for the cash co-payment is ultimately a personal choice. But I've applied it throughout this book to be consistent.

There's another challenge. When checking the equivalent retail airfare to calculate redeemed value, the airline's website can present us with more than one price for the same cabin class on the same flight.

When I researched the first-class airfares from Sydney to Johannesburg there were two fare types, a flexible fare and a more restricted saver fare. My estimate for redeemed value and thereby the Returns will be different depending upon which one I use for my calculation. Which should I select?

Fare classes of purchased airfares can be fully flexible, or non-refundable, or levy significant cash fees, when bookings are changed or cancelled.

Reward seat bookings also have varying flexibility. We can typically change or cancel our booking either for free or at a modest cost depending upon the airline loyalty program, through which we booked the redemption. But some rewards can't be refunded, or are costly to change or cancel.

The consistent approach used in this book is to seek to match the basic terms and conditions of the reward booking to that of the equivalent paid airfare option to estimate the redeemed value of the reward.

That can favor using the higher retail cost of a relatively more flexible fare class to estimate the redeemed value, if the lower airfare has more restrictive conditions than the reward redemption, such as being non-refundable.

Another consideration is whether our reward is for a one-way or return itinerary. Some airfares for one-way itineraries can be significantly more expensive than half the price of a return. Once again, I've mapped the reward to the equivalent airfare to estimate redeemed value.

ACTIONS

If the redemption is for a return itinerary, I've estimated redemption value on the retail airfare for the equivalent return itinerary. If the redemption is for a one-way itinerary, I've calculated redeemed value based upon the retail airfare for the equivalent one-way itinerary.

When constructing our travel itinerary over several one-way reward seat redemptions, we've created flexibility, which itself has value, just as it does for one-way flexible tickets purchased with cash.

Finally, some players make the personal choice to account for the points they would have theoretically earned, if they had bought the airfare rather than redeemed points.

I haven't factored those into the calculation of Returns in this book. That's because by that logic, I should also consider the points, which I could have theoretically earned from the cash that I would have hypothetically saved when redeeming a reward instead of paying cash. Basically, both the cash saved and points earned are notional rather than actual.

The redeemed value of our points can skyrocket from five to even ten or more times greater than the base redeemed value in a given airline loyalty program. We have the opportunity to leverage huge variation in potential Returns.

Furthermore, since redeemed value of our points typically trends upwards with higher cabin class, we can potentially enjoy an elevated travel experience, such as that with priority check-in, lounge access, lie-flat seats, and so forth, through the prudent choice of reward seats.

Our power pack **ENRICH** has six practical actions designed to improve the redeemed value of our redeemed points, whilst elevating our travel experience (see Figure 15).

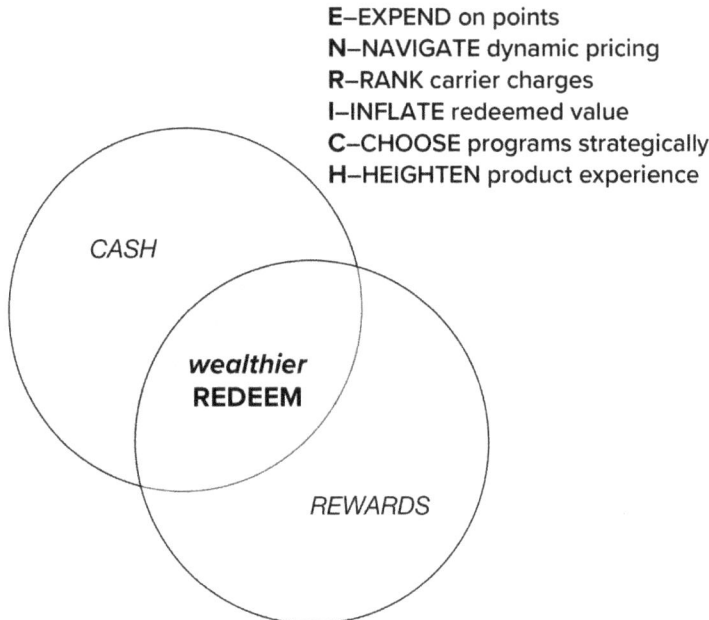

Figure 15: Six actions enrich a wealthier redeem

Let's run through the actions for a wealthier redeem. But I can only put so much detail in one book, so I'll simply outline the core gambits, impacts, and attendant pitfalls. I'll also include how to kick start each action.

Expend on Points

Gambit: airline loyalty programs can offer a facility on their websites to purchase points with cash. Players can use this to top up points totals in their program accounts when just short of the number of points needed for a targeted reward.

Impact: without the top up, we can miss a redemption opportunity, whilst the potential redeemed value of our saved points remains locked up.

ACTIONS

(Anse Source d'Argent, La Digue)

Success - Hong Kong to Seychelles via Dubai
Emirates First Class
(Qantas Frequent Flyer)

POINT BUSTER

Kick start: we can do an online search citing the name of a given airline and the words "purchase points or miles" to track down opportunities to purchase points. There are periodic promotions, offering discounted pricing or bonus points, which are typically headlined and discussed on travel blogs.

We can assess purchase options. Economics buffs can refer to marginal value, the ever-increasing relative benefit of the final batch of points needed to reach our goal. Obviously, this requires some judgement. We don't want to be just 1,000 points short and purchase them at some huge cost because some abstract theory outshone basic common sense.

When making points purchases, players are essentially flipping points to go from cash to redeemed value. A score similar to a Pay-off can guide personal choice.

We can calculate a ***flip score*** by dividing the redeemed value of the points when redeemed, by the cash spent buying the points, times 100.

If the flip score is under 100 percent, there's less redeemed value than the cash expended, arguably a bad deal. If the flip score is over 100 percent, there's more redeemed value than the cash expended, putting us on the right side of the math. Players can decide for themselves where to set the bar. The greater the flip score the better.

Personally, I prefer to set it high, so well above 100 percent, because I'm converting cash into redeemed value and not cash.

Examples: I was about 10,000 miles short in my United Airlines MileagePlus account to be able to redeem two available one-way business class reward seats from Cairns to Singapore, on Singapore Airlines.

Luckily there was a bonus offer. I ran the numbers on purchasing the miles. The flip score was roughly 200 percent, meaning that I'd receive twice as much redeemed value than the cash spent buying the miles. So, I purchased the points to make up the shortfall.

Catch: we can't go back to our cash when buying points, if subject to buyer's remorse. There's a risk when buying points speculatively. Checking reward seat inventory up front can mitigate the risk. But that may or may not coincide with a promotion to purchase points with a bonus. As ever, we need to do the math.

There are alternative ways to top up our points to consider, including transfers from generic credit cards, hotel loyalty and other associated loyalty programs, as available.

Navigate Dynamic Pricing

Gambit: some airline loyalty programs have adopted dynamic pricing models for their reward seats. But players can still identify any competitive redeemed value for their points.

Impact: dynamic pricing can understandably be perceived as negative by players, given the lesser transparency and increased uncertainty compared with traditional reward pricing models. But players can risk missing out on valuable opportunities, if they assume the worst. We can always do the math to reveal attractive redemption opportunities.

Kick start: we can expose that dynamic pricing models apply when there are no award charts or online calculators citing *fixed* numbers of required points for a given redemption.

Some programs, such as Delta SkyMiles, have no award charts at all. Others, such as Alaska Mileage Plan, cite a minimum and others, such as Air Canada Aeroplan, cite a range of required numbers of points for given redemptions.

Dynamic pricing models presenting variable Returns, can be differentiated from Retail-based Rewards, because the former aren't priced solely on the retail value of the equivalent product.

We can check this by running test bookings for reward seats over a range of dates on the website of an airline with dynamic pricing and then compare those data with the equivalent retail cost of the airfares across those dates.

We can always identify the better deals by simply calculating the potential Returns of our redeemed points and considering our overall Pay-off.

We can also identify Award Seats that are still "embedded" in the system, but waiting to be found, by checking availability on the website of a partner program that does still identify Award Seat inventory.

Examples: the United Airlines website is currently offering reward seats ranging from 100,000 to 300,000 points for the single sector itinerary Los Angeles to Sydney in business class. This reveals that dynamic pricing is in play. Furthermore, the retail airfares for the equivalent flights aren't obviously mapping to the number of points required for the redemption.

But the 100,000-points level dynamically priced reward seats match the availability of fixed priced Award Seats available on the website of partner Virgin Australia. We can identify the better deals hidden in the system.

Catch: we don't have the ready convenience of fixed priced award tables to help us to identify the better value reward seat redemptions.

Unless a partial award chart cites the relevant information, we need to summon the effort to do test bookings across a range of dates on the relevant airline's website to research the minimum number of points required for a given reward.

Doing the math to work out potential Returns can guide our choice to accept or reject the variously priced reward seats on offer.

Rank Carrier Charges

Gambit: almost all flyer point redemptions for Award Seats require a cash co-payment. They can cost less than a coffee, or over USD1000 per flight sector. Players can seek to minimize them when they can by choosing the reward option with the lesser cash co-payment.

Impact: cash co-payments can be substantial, especially for premium cabin reward seats, thus creating a cash barrier to our redemption plans and a hit to the redeemed value of our points, not to mention our wallets.

Kick start: purchased airfares have a number of government taxes and airport and other charges included into the cost of the ticket. These fees can be passed onto us or not as part of the cash co-payment of an Award Seat redemption.

There are fee breakdowns on the free website, ITA Matrix by Google, accessed by inputting details of a given flight. These include two-character codes, such as G8 and ZR.

They can include a fee called a Carrier-imposed Surcharge. Some are coded with YQ. The carrying airline imposes such a fee at its own discretion. Airlines that do this include Emirates, Qantas Airways, British Airways, Virgin Atlantic, and Lufthansa, to name just a few. The fee can be included in the cash co-payment when booking an Award Seat.

But not all airline loyalty programs pass on the Carrier-imposed Surcharge when redeeming our points. For example, booking a first-class Award Seat from Bangkok to Dubai on Emirates using our Qantas Frequent Flyer points, currently incurs this fee, depending upon the origin of our itinerary, but redeeming Air Canada Aeroplan points doesn't.

Conversely, some airline loyalty programs, such as Virgin Australia Velocity, appear to levy a cash co-payment, which is not obviously relatable to the carrying airline's listed Carrier-imposed surcharge.

We can do online searches for general trends and examples of how to lessen these cash co-payments, since these are the subject of some travel blog articles.

But to be absolutely sure about the cash co-payment for a given reward seat, we have to do test bookings on the websites of programs' parent airline to extract the data on a case-by case basis in order to compare our options.

Example: redeeming Singapore Airlines KrisFlyer miles for a one-way business class reward seat on Lufthansa from Frankfurt to Mexico City incurs a cash co-payment of about USD675. The cash co-payment falls to about USD190, if redeemed using United Airlines MileagePlus miles instead.

ACTIONS

Catch: we need to put in the effort to research and factor these cash co-payments into our strategic planning. The more flexible our points portfolio, the greater the opportunity to find ways to bypass these charges. Our research needs to take into account not just the typical practice of a given airline loyalty program, but also the specifics of the route and cabin class.

Inflate Redeemed Value

Gambit: the redeemed value of flyer points is only released once players redeem them, and then depends upon the airline loyalty program and the reward itself. Players can inflate the redeemed value of their points by comparing redemption options and choosing the reward offering the better Returns.

Impact: the higher the Returns potentially the greater travel rich reward that players attain for the same everyday spend.

Kick start: we can improve our Returns and thereby our overall Pay-off by selecting our rewards carefully. Quite simply, that means running the math for each redemption option, by calculating the potential Returns for each.

There is typically accelerating value stepping up the cabin classes from economy-coach to first class.

Example: I can redeem my Virgin Australia Velocity points to release Returns of about USD3.25 per 1000 by redeeming them for a gift card, but I've also personally enjoyed roughly 20 times higher Returns by redeeming business class reward seats on partner Singapore Airlines.

Catch: it requires time and effort to search out redemption options and calculate their respective potential Returns.

111

Choose Programs Strategically

Gambit: programs each have their own strengths and sweet spots. Players can choose programs strategically, rather than assess them in isolation, to meet their overall redemption goals.

Impact: adopting a big picture perspective can help to accommodate a broader set of redemption goals.

Kick start: we can consider the strategic benefits of different redemption options in the context of our broader travel goals. This can balance the various program strengths and sweet spots in a way that meets our ongoing needs. We can also consider how easily that we can restock our flyer points redeemed from a given program account.

Examples: I recently flew from Frankfurt to Rome. One-way business class reward seats were available on Lufthansa. I had the options to redeem Singapore Airlines KrisFlyer miles, or United Airlines MileagePlus miles, or avianca life**miles**. The latter required the least number of points and lowest cash co-payment, making that the obvious choice.

But I also considered the options within the bigger picture of my other redemption goals. I prefer to redeem KrisFlyer miles on Singapore Airlines for business and first-class Award Seats, since award availability can be better through KrisFlyer itself than partner programs.

Similarly, I favor redeeming MileagePlus miles on parent United Airline's trans-Pacific flights, since the airlines servicing such routes generally offer only limited availability of Target Rewards.

Catch: without a diversified points portfolio we simply can't empower our gameplay to take a strategic position, because our redemption options are too limited.

Heighten Product Experience

Gambit: different airline products are vastly different, depending upon the route, airline, cabin class, and aircraft configuration. Players can choose to redeem their points for the better product to enrich their travel experience.

Impact: we can redeem our flyer points for a basic economy-coach product versus a premium one offering priority check-in, expedited security and immigration, and a lounge with dining and diverse facilities, an onboard private suite, tasty cuisine and even an on-board shower for first class in the case of the Airbus A380s of Emirates and Etihad.

Kick start: we can track down information on schedule, aircraft, and their configurations. Airlines can display the aircraft type in their booking interface. There are seat maps for given aircraft types on the airline's website and free third-party websites, such as SeatGuru.

We can then use the information on the airline and the aircraft type to make an online search for reviews on travel blogs and social media about the actual product.

Examples: within Europe business class is typically an economy-coach seat with the adjacent seat left empty. The value can shift towards priority check in and security, and lounge access. It's still possible to find lie-flat seats with some sleuthing. Thus, I've traveled on Air Europa's Boeing B787 Dreamliners from Rome to Tenerife via Madrid.

POINT BUSTER

Similarly, the front cabin on domestic flights within the USA can simply be a wider seat with more legroom than economy-coach, rather than a lie-flat, even when branded as first class.

However, I've booked onto an American Airlines Boeing B777 and Hawaiian Airlines Airbus A330 with lie-flat seats on domestic flights within the USA.

Some airlines run their international flights offering potentially elevated product experiences between airports outside of their country of origin, a fifth freedom route. Thus, an Emirates Boeing B777 is currently scheduled between Miami and Bogotá, and an Airbus A380 between Sydney and Christchurch.

Catch: we can plan our itinerary only to find an aircraft swap offers a lessor product. The probability of this happening increases the further ahead that we book.

JUST LIVE IT: enrich a wealthier redeem

(Cathay Pacific Airbus A350, Singapore Changi Airport)

CATHAY PACIFIC FIFTH FREEDOM ROUTE
between BANGKOK and SINGAPORE

STRATEGY

Our flyer points have the capacity to unleash redeemed value, which can vary by up to 10 times or more. But there's a catch. Rewards that deliver richer redeemed value are typically less available and harder to find. We have to improve our odds of successfully finding our goal rewards to unlock greater value.

It's time to reveal a set of supercharging boosters, namely, Flex, Odds, Choice, and Profit, hiding within the three-circle overlaps of the POINT BUSTER (see Figure 16).

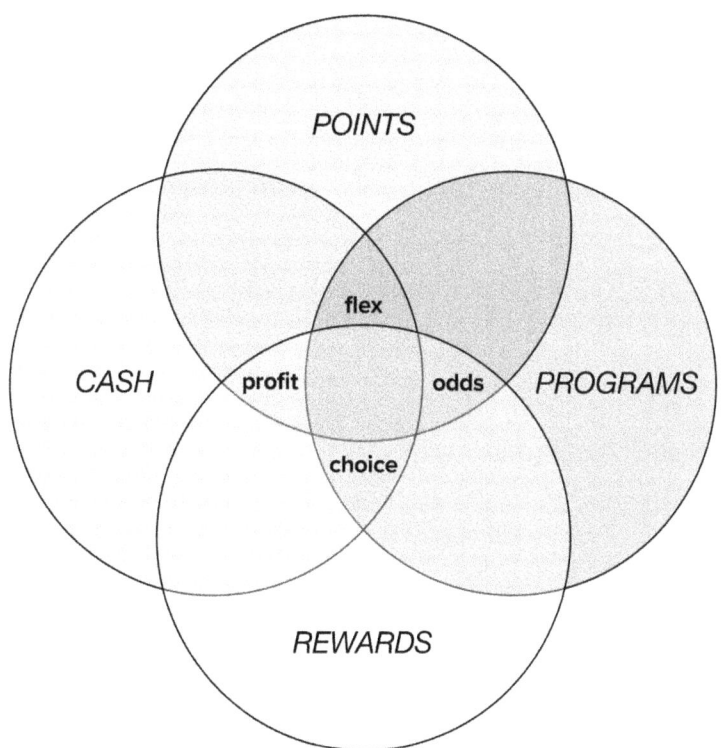

Figure 16: The four hidden boosters

Each booster addresses one of four strategic objectives, namely, to craft greater Flex in our portfolio of points, generate better Odds of successfully finding our goal rewards, drive richer Choice in our selection of rewards, and unlock higher Profit, thus more potential redeemed value for the everyday cash that we spend anyway.

Each booster is created from a combination of two of the power packs from chapter ACTIONS. Remarkably, the actions from one power pack can empower the actions from another in each booster to generate supercharge.

Imagine dropping a Mentos candy into a bottle of Diet Coke only to get soaked in the surging fountains of sticky soda. There are two idle ingredients, which can react wildly when combined.

How can this be? One aspect of our gameplay can impact another. All of the actions are interlinked. Taking control of the relationships between the parts in the system can make our flyer points atomic.

I'm about to explain how that applies for each of our strategic objectives. For example, earning more points per dollar **and** then higher redeemed value per point can empower our Profit. The output of one action power pack accelerates the output of the other to escalate value.

Consider that each player of the flyer point game is in competition with any other who seeks the same goal reward. And each player has their own individual skillset, knowledge, and gameplay. Those players, who boost their points, will potentially have the winning edge amongst the millions of other competing players.

Thus, a player who is more practiced in earning points faster and redeeming wealthier rewards is at a potential advantage over a player of weaker performance. The more adept player is better positioned to unleash richer reward.

For each booster, we'll compare how players applying different strategies can experience varying upside and downside in pursuit of their personal travel goals. We'll see how they can also potentially realign their strategic approach.

Our goal of richer reward will direct our focus onto our **Target Rewards**, Award Seats and Dynamic Rewards, which deliver higher Returns and thereby more redeemed value for our points.

JUST LIVE IT: boost strategic gameplay

(Vaitape, French Polynesia)
Success - Cairns to Papeete via Brisbane and Auckland
Qantas Airways and Air Tahiti Nui Business Class
(Qantas Frequent Flyer)

Flex

Objective: relatively more valuable Target Rewards can be harder to find and players are competing for a limited resource. Our first strategic objective is to boost *Flex*, to manage our points to generate flexibility.

How: we can generate greater Flex by combining our action power packs PROPEL for a faster earn and SECURE for a stronger match. We earn more points *and* then allocate them across multiple program accounts to increase our reward search Options for when we redeem our points (see Figure 17).

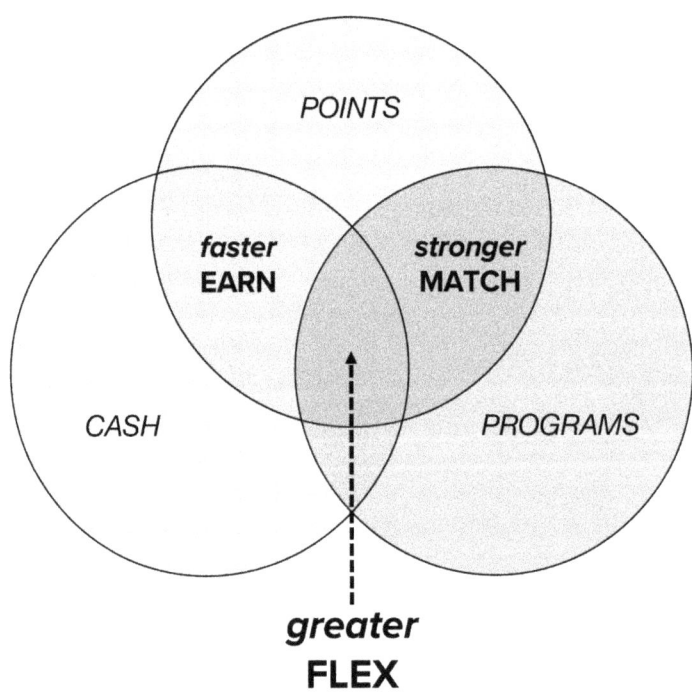

Figure 17: Boost greater FLEX

STRATEGY

Boost: our points have the potential to become ever more flexible in three ways, when grouped in higher numbers.

Firstly, having more points opens up more choice of reward. Secondly, we have more scope to allocate our points strategically across different program accounts. Thirdly, more choice and greater program diversity extend our opportunity to select Target Rewards of greater redeemed value.

Let's work through a very simple hypothetical example of saving up to 120,000 points to illustrate their shifting powers. An airline loyalty program offers Target Reward seats in economy-coach for 30,000 points with a redeemed value of USD300, business class for 60,000 points with a redeemed value of USD1500, and in first class for 120,000 points and a redeemed value of USD6000 (see Figure 18).

Number of points – total redeemed value

120,000 - USD6000			
60,000 - USD1500		60,000 - USD1500	
60,000 - USD1500		30,000 - USD300	30,000 - USD300
30,000 - USD300	30,000 - USD300	30,000 - USD300	30,000 - USD300

Figure 18: Hypothetical reward options for 120,000 points

Let's assume that we save our points from scratch. With 30,000 points saved, we can redeem one economy-coach reward seat, unlocking USD10 redeemed value per 1000 points. But with 60,000 points saved, we can snare one business-class reward seat delivering USD25 redeemed value per 1000 points. The value of our points has jumped 2.5 times.

119

Finally, with 120,000 points saved, we can redeem a first-class reward seat delivering USD50 redeemed value per 1000 points. The value of our points has now potentially jumped by 5 times.

In this scenario, more redeemed value is unleashed by saving and grouping our points into larger batches. Our points become potentially more powerful the more that we accrue.

This pattern typically holds true in real-life. There are exceptions to the trend, but these form program sweet spots of potential advantage to our gameplay.

Now there's a problem. More valuable reward seats are in limited supply and harder to find. Dividing our points across multiple programs, generates more reward search Options for when we want to redeem our points for our goal reward.

Let's continue our hypothetical example and assume that we can divide 120,000 points across up to four programs, with each offering the same reward seat options as above.

When targeting a reward at 120,000 points, there can only be one batch of points in the one program to access our reward and thereby minimal flexibility.

But when targeting a reward at 60,000 points, there can be up to two batches of points in two different programs to access our reward and thereby some flexibility.

Finally, when targeting a reward at 30,000 points, there can be up to four batches of points in up to four different programs to access our reward and thereby the most flexibility.

Road block - we need to allocate smaller batches of points across multiple accounts for higher flexibility versus bigger batches to access Target Rewards of higher redeemed value.

STRATEGY

Obviously, our scenario is simplistic. In reality, we need to plan for flexibility up front, since program selection is typically locked in when earning points.

Strategic counter-plays include seeking to break out of being limited by numbers of points, as we'll explore in chapter JUICE. We can also add generic credit cards into the mix to enable the flexible transfer of our card points to our airline loyalty program accounts as needed.

Examples: I planned a trip from Australia to French Polynesia and had some flexibility in travel dates. I started by searching for reward seats from Auckland to Papeete, since this sector has the least availability. Two airlines served the route, namely, Air Tahiti Nui and Air New Zealand.

There were other more complex routings to reach Papeete, such as those including the Hawaiian Airlines service from Honolulu, that would have encouraged me to rethink the trip as a two-center vacation to fit reward seat availability.

My points portfolio was sufficiently flexible to access any available Target Reward seats. I could redeem Qantas Frequent Flyer points or American AAdvantage miles on Air Tahiti Nui and Qantas Airways. Alternatively, I could redeem my Singapore Airlines KrisFlyer miles or my United MileagePlus miles or avianca life**miles** on Air New Zealand.

In the event there were Award Seats in business class available on Air Tahiti Nui and connecting flights on Qantas Airways outbound. I simply bought tickets for the returning flights on Air Zealand from Papeete to Cairns, given a relatively cheap business class promotional fare. It doesn't make sense to use the points when they offer low redeemed value, but rather pay with cash.

Strategy: let's explore four strategies, which impact the flexibility of flyer points. I've simply defined these by whether a player achieves a slow or fast point earn, and whether they engage with one or multiple programs (see Figure 19).

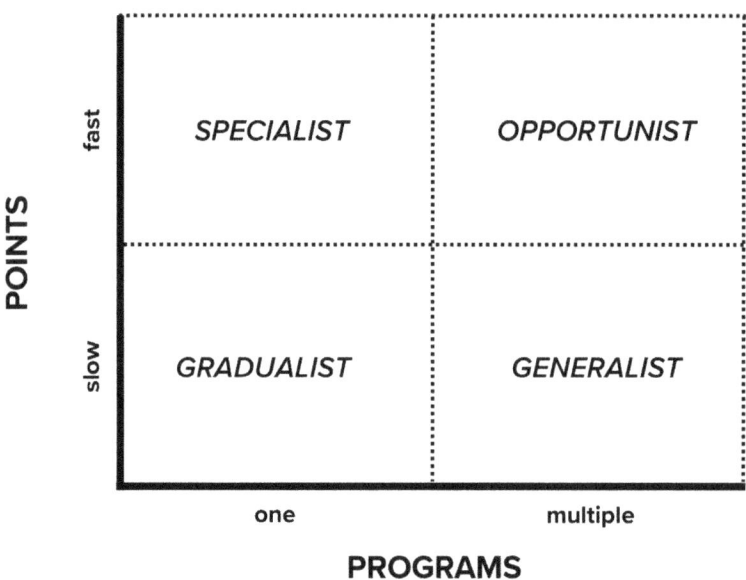

Figure 19: Strategies impacting FLEX

Strategy **Gradualist** is simply to earn points when making a purchase. This strategy only requires the player to be a member of at least one airline loyalty program. Points are earned incidentally as part of the transaction and Earn Rates can be relatively slow.

One example would be when a player earns points for any everyday spend without chasing down elevated Earn Rates and bonus offers. Another example would be when a player earns points by making purchases with a co-branded credit card at a base rate of just one or several points per USD.

The upside of strategy Gradualist is that it requires very little effort. The player can easily earn points from the cash that they'd be spending anyway with program partners and also by using a co-branded credit card, whether or not a retailer is a program partner.

The downside of this strategy is that points accrue slowly. Unless they spend big cash, the player only generates a low number of total points and thereby poor flexibility. Being locked into just the one airline loyalty program also limits the number of search Options that match with the player's Target Rewards.

Strategy **Generalist** is to earn flyer points whenever possible from any everyday spend. This strategy requires the player to engage with multiple airline loyalty programs to extend the scope of cash transactions that can earn points, even though Earn Rates can be relatively slow.

One example is when an everyday shopper aims to take advantage of any opportunity to earn loyalty points when they make purchases, regardless of the program.

Another example is when a player earns points through their employment, but is restricted to the best airfare of the day in economy-coach. They earn points from more than one airline and are active in multiple airline loyalty programs.

The upside of strategy Generalist is that the player can earn their points across partners of multiple airline loyalty programs. They can favor spend on a generic credit card and transfer their card points to any allied airline loyalty program.

By engaging with multiple programs, the player can generate flexibility by increasing the number of search Options that match with their Target Rewards.

The downside of this strategy is that flexibility is restricted by total number of points, unless the player is spending big cash to earn their points. The player only has sufficient points to be able to redeem a limited set of rewards.

The player needs to balance how their total points are spread across their airline loyalty program accounts. Engaging with multiple programs promotes flexibility, but dilutes the number of points in any given program.

Unlocking flexibility requires some planning and effort. The player needs to assign their non card earn to one of their airline loyalty programs as they spend their cash with a given program partner and then decide when and how to allocate their generic credit card points.

Strategy **Specialist** is to earn the points of just one airline loyalty program and to do that well. This strategy requires a player to become familiar with the one program and adept at searching out elevated Earn Rates to accrue their points fast.

One example is when an everyday shopper makes regular purchases with specific retailers allied to a given airline loyalty program and seeks out bonus point offers to earn their points.

They exploit sign up bonuses for co-branded credit cards and earn flyer points for any transaction, whether or not the supplier is a partner of their chosen airline loyalty program.

Another example would be when a player earns points through just one program through their employment, because they are expected to travel on the airline loyalty program's parent and allied partner airlines. They may also live or work near an airport, which is a hub for a program's parent or allied airline, making that program an obvious choice.

STRATEGY

The upside of strategy Specialist is that the player can focus their time, effort, and expertise onto the one program. They can harness any program strengths and relatively higher Earn Rates to accrue their points faster.

The player can amass point totals that increase flexibility of reward choice. Their points are earned fast and concentrated into the one program account. In some programs, they can pool points from members of a family, or household, or defined group.

They can seek to gain status in their chosen program to benefit from tier features, such as upgrade priority, which they personally perceive to be of value.

The downside of this strategy is that the player misses out on the flexibility generated by engaging with more than the one program. This can restrict the number of search Options that match with their Target Rewards.

Finally, strategy **Opportunist** is to earn the most points for a given everyday cash spend across multiple airline loyalty programs. This strategy requires the player to increase the proportion of their everyday cash spend that earns points and also to favor transactions offering relatively higher Earn Rates.

Engaging with multiple airline loyalty programs generates more reward search Options that match with the player's Target Rewards.

One example is when a canny shopper seeks out the best bonus points offers across multiple loyalty platforms. They churn and carry multiple generic credit cards and select the card which offers the better Earn Rate given the spend category, be that travel, or dining, or groceries, and so forth.

Another example would be a very frequent flyer, who travels on multiple airlines. They allocate their points to the program that offers the best point earn for their airfare spend.

The upside of this strategy is that the player can quickly amass high numbers of points. This generates greater flexibility and thereby reward choice in addition to more search Options. The player can transfer their generic credit card points flexibly to multiple airline loyalty programs. The downside is that this all demands knowledge, skill, and effort.

Take outs: strategy Opportunist is theoretically the optimal approach to boost greater flexibility. In practice, we simply combine action pack PROPEL to earn points faster, with action pack SECURE to engage with multiple programs.

Higher points totals increase choice of reward. We can also allocate our points strategically across different program accounts. Greater program diversity increases the number of search Options that match with our Target Rewards.

How can we improve upon the suboptimal strategies of Gradualist, Generalist, and Specialist?

Strategy Gradualist is both points and programs poor. We can address that by applying the actions in power pack PROPEL to earn points faster in combination with those in power pack SECURE to engage with multiple programs.

Strategy Generalist is points poor. We can apply action power pack PROPEL to earn points faster.

Strategy Specialist is programs poor. We can apply action pack SECURE to engage with multiple programs.

In reality, the definitions and application of the four strategies are fluid. In practice, we can adopt any one at any time.

STRATEGY

Thus, sometimes we might accept relatively slow point earn to avoid missing out on earning points.

At other times we might choose to focus on a specific program, for example, because reward seats in business or first class are preferentially released to that program's own members.

JUST LIVE IT: boost greater Flex

(Singapore Airlines Boeing B737, Darwin International Airport)

Success - Darwin to Frankfurt via Singapore
Singapore Airlines Business Class
(Virgin Airlines Velocity)

Odds

Objective: our second strategic objective is to boost our *Odds*, to make it more likely to find those Target Rewards that are available.

We're seeking to outwit the trend that rewards offering relatively greater redeemed value are less likely to be available and thereby harder to find. Our search skills can also give us the edge to find available rewards before competing players.

How: we can boost better Odds by combining the actions from our power packs SECURE for a stronger match and MASTER for a smarter search (see Figure 20).

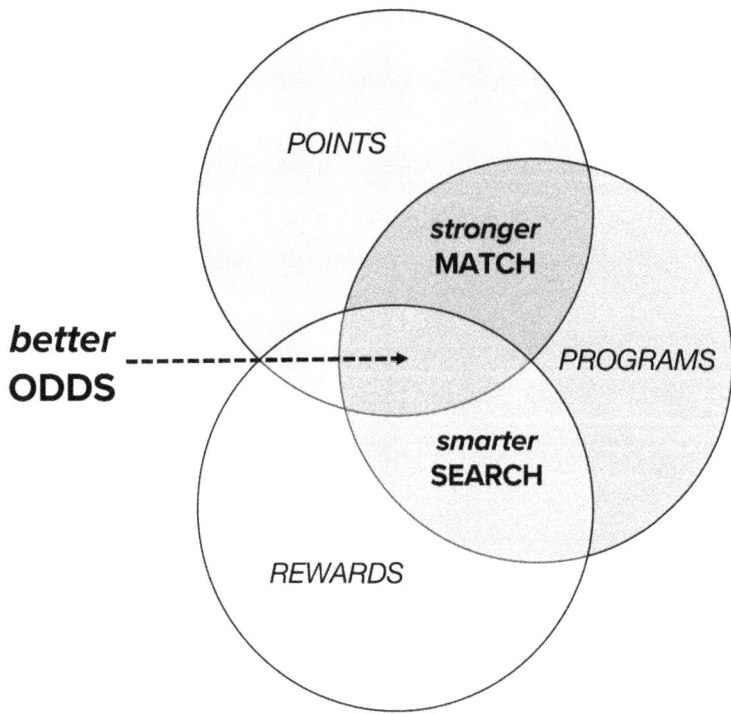

Figure 20: Boost better ODDS

STRATEGY

Boost: we can create a boost when we increase the number of flights searched and also elevate our Chances of finding available Target Rewards, by improving our search skills.

Firstly, increasing flight search Options opens up our access to available Target Rewards. When we search one flight there are two possible outcomes, either at least one Target Reward or none.

But the possible combinations escalate exponentially thereafter. Searching three flights delivers eight combinations, and four flights sixteen combinations, and so forth.

Remarkably, however many flight Options searched, all but one combination delivers at least one Target Reward. Thus, seven of eight combinations deliver at least one Target Reward, when searching three flights (see Figure 21).

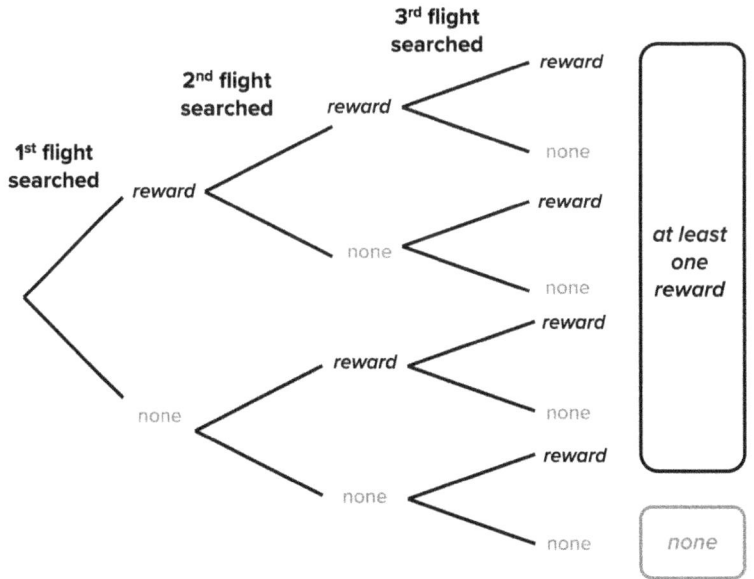

Figure 21: Search combinations escalate exponentially

What's the catch? We also have to factor in the probability of each outcome. The availability of reward seats isn't constant. One in economy-coach can be much more common and easier to find that one in business class.

Thus, the probability of a Target Reward on any given flight search Option is variable. In short, that means that the combinations will not be equally likely.

In practice, there is an interplay between the number of flight search Options, thereby the number of combinations, and also the probability that a Target Reward is available on any given flight search Option.

For the math savvy only, I ran the numbers in a very simple combinations model, assuming equally distributed Target Rewards, and compared the Chances of Target Rewards on any given flight search Options set at both 1 in 10 (0.10) and 1 in 20 (or 0.05) (see Figure 22).

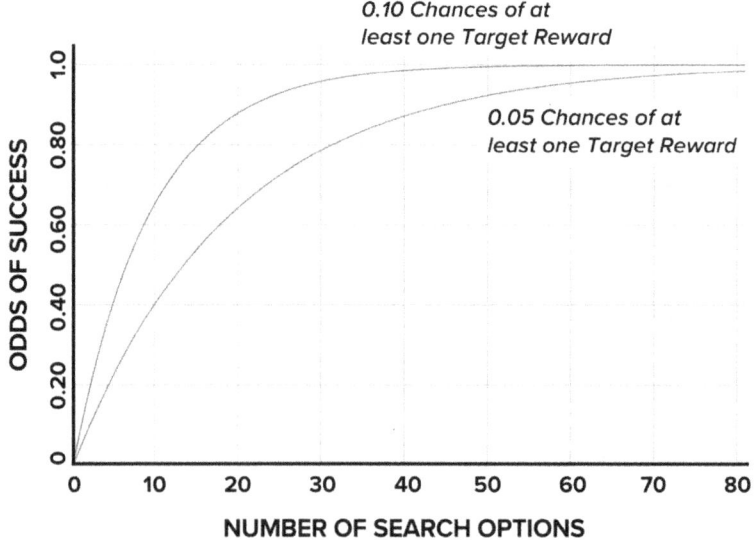

Figure 22: Search Options drive Odds of success

The simple practical message is that we can elevate our Odds of success by offsetting low Target Reward availability with increasing numbers of flight search Options, even when Target Rewards are hard to find.

Secondly, we can seek to increase our Chances of finding those Target Rewards that are available. Imagine that there are four available spread across 20 flights, but we can only find two of them. We can potentially reveal double the number of Target Rewards by improving our reward search skills.

Luckily, we can be shrewd in our search and be ahead of the curve by exploiting patterns of reward seat release. For example, airlines can add a flight to the schedule and offer a fresh batch of reward seats. Some airlines release unsold inventory as reward seats close to the date of travel.

Examples: I wanted to get home to Australia in business or first class after visiting family in Los Angeles. The preferred route was a non-stop flight to Sydney. There were four airlines servicing that route, namely, Delta Air Lines, United Airlines, American Airlines, and Qantas Airways.

My points portfolio had the flexibility to redeem Target Reward seats from the once daily flights of any of those airlines. I could travel across a date range of 5 days, thereby generating 4 times 5, thus 20 flight search Options.

I applied a couple of tricks to elevate my overall Odds of success. I booked an itinerary on a less preferred route as a back stop. I stayed flexible and kept checking Target Reward availability. Target Rewards were released close to the date of travel. I was able to rebook my travel by redeeming Alaska Mileage Plan miles for two business class reward seats, when Qantas Airways added an extra weekly flight.

Strategy: let's explore four strategies, which impact the Odds of successfully searching out our Target Rewards. I've simply defined these by whether a player engages with one or multiple programs and whether their capacity to search out Target Rewards is basic or skilled (see Figure 23).

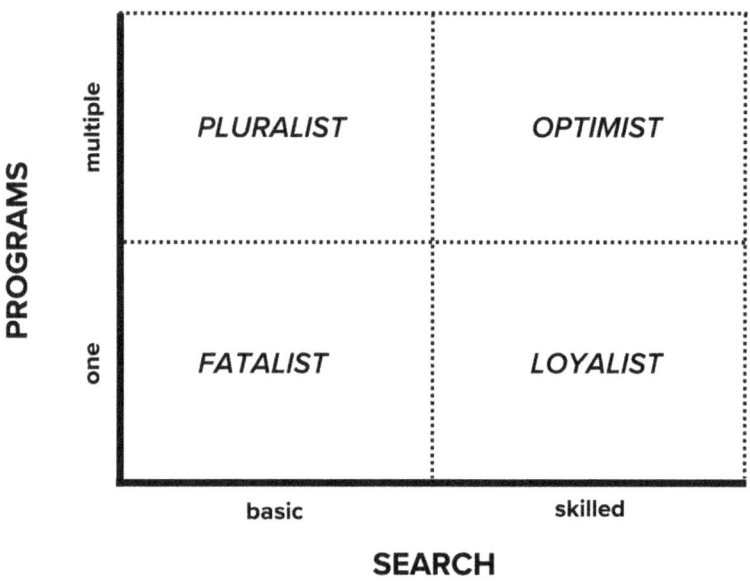

Figure 23: Strategies impacting ODDS

Strategy **Fatalist** is to set modest reward goals that can be easily met. This strategy simply requires that the player belong to at least one airline loyalty program and redeem their flyer points for rewards that are readily available.

One example is when a player is an incidental collector of flyer points, when spending their cash through one airline loyalty program's retail partners. They take the points that are on offer, rather than leave them behind. They perceive points to be free and any reward a bonus.

STRATEGY

They have little motivation to develop their reward search skills or engage with multiple programs, because they redeem their points for very accessible rewards, such as a gift voucher, merchandise, or to offset the cash cost of a hotel room or airfare using a points-plus-pay facility.

Another example is when a player becomes demotivated when they can't find rewards that satisfy their redemption goals. They lower their expectations. Thereafter, they take the path of least effort and don't bother to mature their reward search skills or engage with multiple programs.

The upside of strategy Fatalist is that there are high Odds of successfully finding rewards of high availability, given easily achievable reward goals. The strategy requires minimal effort. The player can view any redeemed reward as a bonus over and above the products purchased when earning points.

The downside is that the Fatalist is potentially missing out on the opportunity to access a broader selection of rewards. A small improvement in their search skills or joining more programs hold the potential to transform their overall Odds of successfully revealing available Target Rewards, rather than Dynamic Rewards and Retail-based Rewards of relatively lesser redeemed value.

Strategy **Pluralist** is to access available Target Rewards across multiple programs. This strategy requires that a player engage in several programs, but not necessarily develop their reward search skills.

One example is when a player uses a generic credit card to amass points through their everyday spend. They can transfer card points to one of many airline loyalty programs to access any available Targets Rewards offered by those programs.

However, they haven't developed their reward search skills, because doing so for the many allied airline loyalty programs of their credit card is daunting and requires effort.

Another example is when a player's employer adopts a travel policy of best fare on the day across multiple airlines. The player ends up with points across several airline loyalty programs. They also make retail purchase through the online malls offered by those programs to accrue their points totals.

Their search skills aren't sufficiently advanced to identify Award Seats or compare the redeemed value of different Dynamic Rewards. They simply redeem the points of whichever airline loyalty program offers their goal redemption for the least number of points.

The upside of strategy Pluralist is that a player can enjoy access to reward seats across multiple programs.

The downside is that whereas the player has pursued program diversity, the resulting flexibility can only be fully released by maturing their reward search skills. Having only basic skills restricts their access to available Target Rewards offering relatively greater redeemed value than more readily available Dynamic Rewards and retail-based Rewards.

Strategy **Loyalist** is to access any Target Rewards available through the one airline loyalty program. This strategy requires the player to mature their search skills within just that one program.

One example is when a player leverages their business cash flow to meet their personal travel goals, rather than spend their own personal cash. They earn the points of a local loyalty program, which caters for business members.

STRATEGY

The opportunity for personal gain from their business spend encourages them to develop their Target Reward search skills. They are familiar with the airline, its routes, product, website booking interface, and typical patterns of reward seat availability and release.

They can seek to gain status in their chosen program to benefit from tier features that they personally perceive to be of value.

The upside of the Loyalist strategy is that a player can improve their Chances of finding their Target Rewards, whilst at a potential advantage over less seasoned players seeking to redeem the same Target Rewards. They can access any Target Rewards released by the program's parent airline preferentially to its own members, whereas members of the program of an allied airline cannot redeem those rewards.

The downside is that a player can only access the available Target Rewards of just the one airline loyalty program. That limits the number of search Options that match their Target Rewards and thereby reduces their Odds of successfully meeting their redemption goals.

Finally, strategy **Optimist** is to access any available Target Rewards. The goal is to outsmart the challenge of limited Target Reward availability as far as practically possible. This strategy requires the player to engage with multiple airline loyalty programs and mature their skills at searching for Target Rewards across all of those programs.

The player needs the confidence and capacity to confront the risks of the game and have a positive attitude towards their Odds of successfully redeeming their Target Rewards.

POINT BUSTER

One example is when a player actively earns points across the full scope of their everyday spend through multiple airline loyalty programs. They set their redemption goals, and plan and manage their portfolio of points and programs to increase the reward search Options that match with their Target Rewards. They use a generic credit card and transfer card points flexibly to their favored airline loyalty programs as required.

They develop their search skills across multiple programs, being fully aware that more valuable Target Rewards are in limited supply and that they are in competition with other players for the same reward seats.

Another example is when a very frequent flyer engages with multiple airlines and their respective allied airline program partners. They develop their search skills across their chosen programs. They are already very familiar with routes, products, website booking interface, and typical patterns of reward seat availability and release for multiple airlines.

The upside of strategy Optimist is that the player can open up the broadest access to available Target Rewards. This in turn increases the number of search Options that match their Target Rewards, whilst improving their Chances of finding those rewards and doing so before a competing player.

The downside is that the player needs to put in the time and effort to upskill, and to familiarize themselves with the strengths and quirks of a number of airlines' booking interfaces. They need to keep up to date with program changes and develop their awareness of patterns of reward seat availability.

STRATEGY

Take outs: strategy Optimist is theoretically the optimal strategy to boost better Odds of successfully finding our goal Target Rewards. In practice, we simply combine action pack SECURE to engage with multiple programs, with action pack MASTER to improve our skills at revealing available Target Rewards.

Greater program diversity increases our Odds of success. We can aim to generate more flight search Options that match with our Target Rewards. We'll need a mixed portfolio of program accounts, potentially backed up with a generic credit card from which to transfer points flexibly as needed.

We can also elevate our Odds of success by improving our skillset and thereby our Chances of searching out Target Rewards that are waiting to be found and doing so before a competing player. Basically, we don't want to miss a redemption opportunity.

Harnessing more flight search Options ***and*** revealing more Target Rewards that are available and waiting to be found can unlock the broadest possible access to Target Rewards.

How can we improve upon the suboptimal strategies of Fatalist, Loyalist, and Pluralist?

Basically, strategy Fatalist is both skills poor and programs poor. We can address that by applying the actions in power pack SECURE to engage with multiple programs and power pack MASTER to improve our skills at revealing available Target Rewards.

Strategy Pluralist is skills poor. We can apply actions power pack MASTER to improve our skills at revealing available Target Rewards.

POINT BUSTER

Finally, strategy Loyalist is programs poor. We can apply action power pack SECURE to engage with multiple programs.

In reality, the definitions and application of the four strategies are fluid. In practice, any player can adopt any one at any time. Thus, we'll face situations in which our selection of multiple airline loyalty programs is hindered by limiting factors, such as the ease of earning and restocking our flyer points in any given program.

Likewise, our search skills will be less relevant when the program typically releases Target Rewards close to the departure date of the flight, but we can't travel at short notice.

JUST LIVE IT: boost better Odds

(Delta Connection Embraer E-175, San José Mineta International Airport)

POSITIONING FLIGHT to LOS ANGELES
LINKING REWARD SEAT REDEMPTIONS

STRATEGY

Choice

Objective: when players are fresh at the flyer point game, they can feel relief just to be able to redeem their points for a reward seat. But developing their gameplay skills can increasingly satisfy their travel goals *and* unlock greater travel rich reward. Our third strategic objective is to boost richer Choice. We can generate a greater selection of rewards from which to choose, and select one of higher redeemed value.

How: we can boost richer Choice by combining our power packs MASTER for a smarter search and ENRICH for a wealthier redeem (see Figure 24).

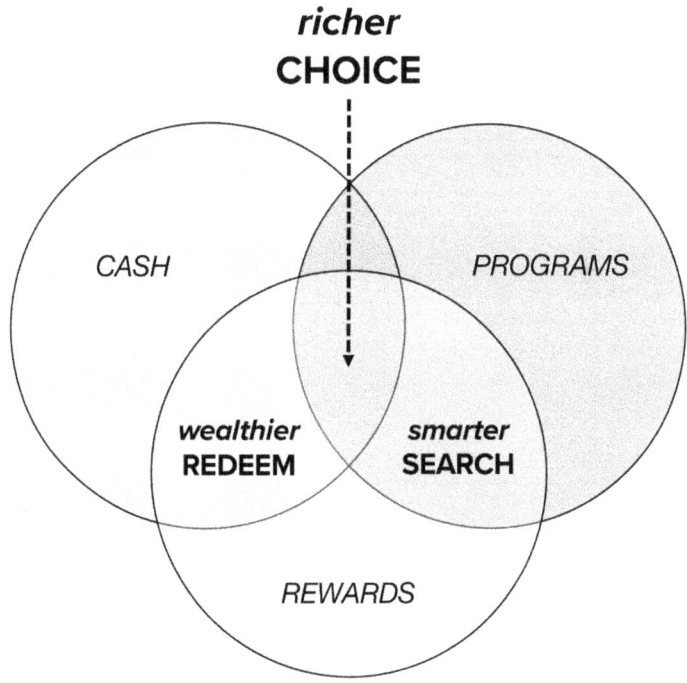

Figure 24: Boost richer CHOICE

Boost: we can boost richer Choice by aiming to increase the number of Target Rewards that we can access and then selecting the more valuable reward.

But rewards offering greater redeemed value are less available and therefore less likely. We need to uncover more reward seats to increase our Odds of successfully finding one from which to choose.

Let's illustrate that hypothetically using idealized data loosely based upon real life airline loyalty programs. I've plotted the probability of finding a reward seat on any given flight searched against their respective Returns, if redeemed (see Figure 25).

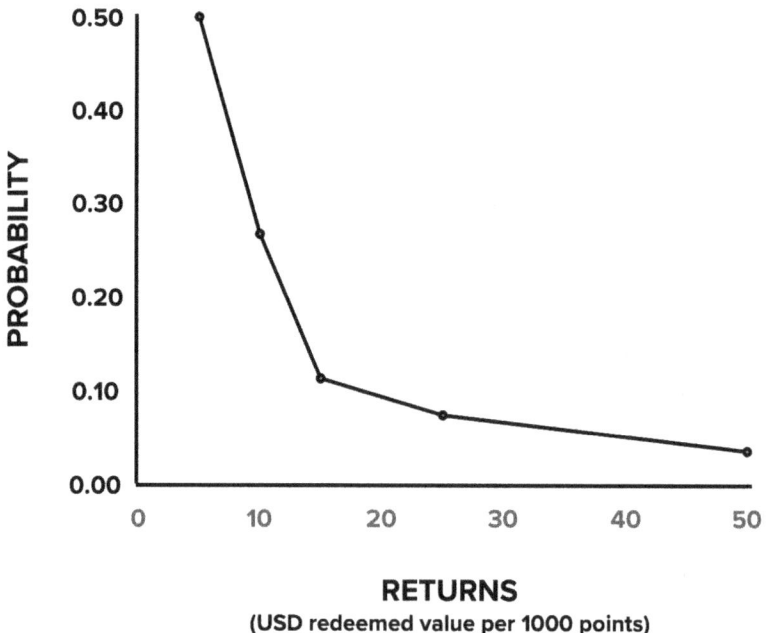

Figure 25: Higher Returns are less likely

The curve falls away to the right. Basically, reward seats offering USD5 per 1000 points are the most likely. They are the easiest to find. Reward seats offering USD50 per 1000 points are least likely. That are much harder to find.

Our ability to search out more Target Rewards initially depends upon how well that we've played the flyer point game thus far to accrue points, empower them with flexibility, and allocate them across multiple airline loyalty programs.

Then our search skills kick in, so that we can reveal those reward seats that are available from which to select our reward redemption. Our choice can in turn be guided by the redeemed value potentially delivered by those reward seats that we've found.

Examples: I harvested data over a 100-day period based upon using AAdvantage miles for a one-way flight from Los Angeles to Sydney on American Airlines.

I counted the number of flights offering at least one reward seat in different cabin classes. Since AAdvantage reward seats are Dynamic Rewards, I only scored those at the minimum required points for first, business and economy-coach respectively. I also checked the retail price of a one-way flight to estimate redeemed value and thereby calculate Returns.

The business class reward seats offered about 2.7 times and the first class about 8 times better Returns than the economy-coach redemptions. But the business class rewards were about 10 times less available and the first-class rewards about 20 times less available than the economy-coach rewards.

This fits the general pattern. Reward seats delivering higher redeemed value are harder to find. We need a smarter search and a wealthier redeem to boost richer Choice.

POINT BUSTER

Strategy: let's explore four strategies, which impact the richness of Choice of our rewards. I've simply defined these by whether a player achieves poor or rich Returns, and whether they redeem few or many rewards (see Figure 26).

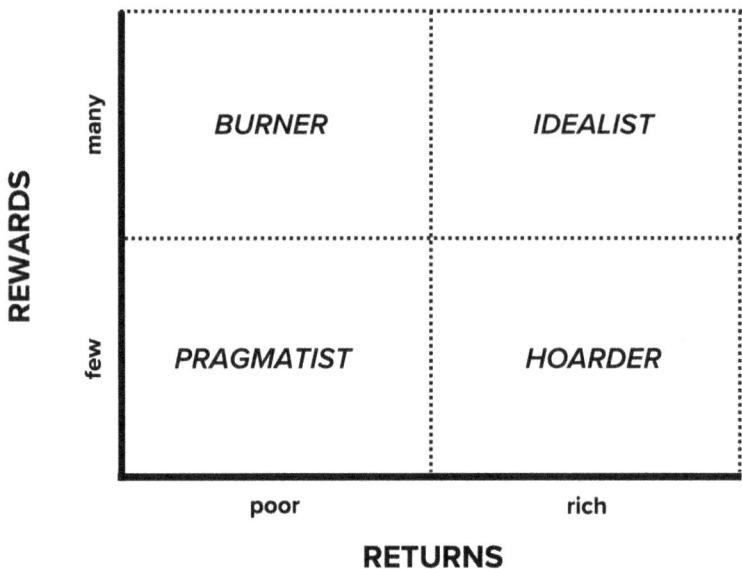

Figure 26: Strategies impacting CHOICE

Strategy **Pragmatist** is to redeem flyer points to satisfy an individual travel need or want regardless of redeemed value. This strategy only requires that a player save flyer points and have an immediate travel need, which can be addressed by redeeming those flyer points. The player accepts choices, which are relatively redemption value poor.

An example is when a shopper accrues points from everyday spend. Their reward goal is for return domestic flights in economy-coach to visit family once a year in another city. The availability of reward seats offering greater redeemed value is of minor consequence.

STRATEGY

Although they could potentially unlock more redeemed value or enjoy more rewards, they have already met their most compelling travel need with the one annual redemption.

The upside of strategy Pragmatist is that a player can feel that they have extracted value from their flyer points, by addressing their individual travel need or want.

Their approach is very practical in that it can satisfy a goal with relative certainty, because a reward of relatively low redeemed value tends to be readily available and easy to find.

The player doesn't need to perform in the flyer point game at a level that advances their access to more rewards or Target Rewards offering relatively rich Returns.

The downside is that the player risks missing the opportunity to satisfy more ambitious travel goals. They redeem relatively fewer rewards to address immediate needs and risk bypassing the opportunity to seek out more bang for buck, whilst also satisfying their redemption goals.

Strategy **Burner** is to redeem the most rewards for a given number of flyer points. This strategy requires that the player is adept at the flyer point game. They take advantage of relatively higher point earn and focus on their ability to accrue points fast.

The player accepts choices, which are relatively redemption value poor. They opt for more rewards, thereby favoring rewards in economy-coach, which require less points than those in premium cabin classes.

One example is when a parent redeems points for their daughter to travel repeatedly to and from college in another city from home. Another example is when a globetrotter seeks to visit as many places as possible.

POINT BUSTER

The upside of strategy Burner is that a player can make more reward redemptions for the same number of total points. That can still meet their travel goals, if they personally value quantity over quality, or in this case, are content to sit in economy-coach rather than business class. Their preferred economy-coach reward seats are easier to find than those in premium cabin classes.

The downside is that they can limit their opportunity to unlock more bang for buck for their original cash spend.

Strategy **Hoarder** is to save flyer points to redeem for a dream trip sometime in the distant future. This strategy requires that a player redeems their points relatively infrequently, but are able to seek out relatively rich Returns to travel in stye and comfort. The player seeks choices, which are relatively redemption value rich.

An example is when an employee travels extensively for work. They save their points for a trip taken during their long service leave or during retirement. They favor rewards in business or first class. They are content to redeem few flights, but target more redeemed value for their points.

The upside of strategy Hoarder is that a player can access greater redeemed value for the same number of total points. They personally value quality over quantity.

The downside is that the player can miss opportunities to enjoy more reward flights for their original cash spend. Their points can also devalue before they are redeemed.

Finally, strategy **Idealist** is to redeem flyer points for choices, which are relatively redemption value rich, without limitation on the number of flights redeemed for a given number of flyer points.

This strategy requires that a player be very practised and committed to the flyer point game. One example is when a player collects points through their work travel and everyday spend. They accrue flyer points across multiple programs and in sufficient numbers to unlock the flexibility of their points.

They have matured reward search skills and thereby full access to available Target Rewards that match with their travel goals. They are competent at calculating redeemed value, so can compare available reward options and thereby select Target Rewards offering richer Choice.

The upside of strategy Idealist is that a player can choose from a full scope of available Target Rewards. They can select the one offering the better bang for buck, whilst satisfying their travel goals. They are more likely to be able to redeem more comfortable Target Rewards in business or first class.

The downside is that a player has to commit to considerable ongoing effort. They ultimately have no control over the availability of Reward Seat released by the airlines.

Take outs: strategy Idealist is theoretically the optimal approach to boost richer Choice. In practice, we simply combine action power pack MASTER to improve our skills at revealing available Target Rewards, with ENRICH to redeem more value per point.

How can we improve upon the suboptimal strategies of Pragmatist, Burner, and Hoarder?

Strategy Pragmatist is poor in both rewards and Returns. We can address that by applying the actions in power pack MASTER to improve our skills at revealing available Target Rewards, with those in power pack ENRICH to redeem more value per point.

POINT BUSTER

Strategy Burner is Returns poor. We can apply action power pack ENRICH to redeem more value per point. Finally, strategy Hoarder is rewards poor. We can apply action power pack MASTER to improve our skills at revealing available Target Rewards.

In reality, the definitions and application of the four strategies are fluid. In practice, any player can adopt any one at any time. Thus, we'll face situations in which we'd rather take more flights and accept less redeemed value, or choose to prioritize redeemed value over numbers of flights, or select a reward of poor redeemed value simply to use up a relatively small number of points orphaned in one of our airline loyalty program accounts.

JUST LIVE IT: boost richer Choice

(Onboard Cathay Pacific Airbus A350 business class)

RIDE THE NUMBERS

STRATEGY

Profit

Objective: we risk missing most of the action, when solely focused upon the redeemed value of our flyer points. We also need to address the ease of earning those points in the first place. Then we can target unleashing more value.

Our fourth strategic objective is to boost our ***Profit***, how much redeemed value our points can potentially deliver for our cash spend.

How: we can drive higher Profit by combining the actions from power pack PROPEL for a faster earn and those from power pack ENRICH for a wealthier redeem (see Figure 27).

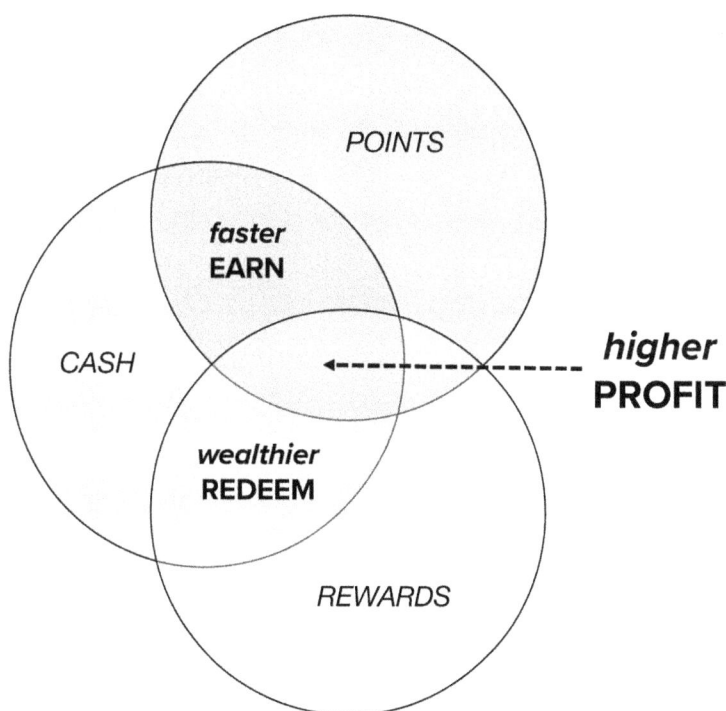

Figure 27: Boost higher PROFIT

We can calculate our Profit by simply multiplying our Earn Rate by our Returns. Dividing by 10 aligns the units. For the math savvy, that's because Returns are quoted per 1000 points and the aim is to arrive at a percentage score.

Let's practice. An Earn Rate of 5 points per USD combined with Returns of USD20 redeemed value per 1000 points delivers a Profit score of 5 times 20 divided by 10, thus 10 percent. If achieved, that would unlock USD10 redeemed value for a USD100 spend earning points.

But I've already defined a measure of objective value, the Pay-off. Why the need for both? Our Pay-off is only realized when a reward is available and we redeem our points. Our Profit score is any theoretical combination of Earn Rate and Returns, regardless of reward availability.

Profit and Pay-off will be the same, if and when we successfully redeem a reward and lock in a given combination of actual real-life Earn Rate and Returns.

For the math savvy, the equation for Profit above is simply an extended version of that for Pay-off (redeemed value divided by cash spend times 10) given reward availability.

Boost: we can boost Profit, because any step up in Earn Rate multiplies any step up in Returns. We can easily explore the accelerating impact of combining a faster earn with a wealthier redeem with a simple times table.

I've recast a times table as a Profit score table. The horizontal axis represents the Earn Rate and the vertical axis represents Returns, across a commonly experienced range of up to 24 points per USD and USD24 redeemed value per 1000 points respectively. Both axes jump two units at a time to fit in this book (see Figure 28).

STRATEGY

RETURNS (USD redeemed value per 1000 points)											*profit score (%)*
24	5	10	14	19	24	29	34	38	43	48	53	58
22	4	9	13	18	22	26	31	35	40	44	48	53
20	4	8	12	16	20	24	28	32	36	40	44	48
18	4	7	11	14	18	22	25	29	32	36	40	43
16	3	6	10	13	16	19	22	26	29	32	35	38
14	3	6	8	11	14	17	20	22	25	28	31	34
12	2	5	7	10	12	14	17	19	22	24	26	29
10	2	4	6	8	10	12	14	16	18	20	22	24
8	2	3	5	6	8	10	11	13	14	16	18	19
6	1	2	4	5	6	7	8	10	11	12	13	14
4	<1	2	2	3	4	5	6	6	7	8	9	10
2	<1	<1	1	2	2	2	3	3	4	4	4	5
	2	4	6	8	10	12	14	16	18	20	22	24

EARN RATE (points per USD)

Figure 28: Earn Rate and Returns drive Profit

I've populated the Profit scores by multiplying the various combinations of numbers from along the two axes and adjusted the units by dividing by 10. I've rounded to the nearest whole number and *"<1"* means less than one.

The table captures the spread of theoretical Profit scores obtainable within that range of Earn Rate and Returns. If we can secure an Earn Rate of 4 points per USD and then redeem those points with Returns of USD20 redeemed value per 1000 points, we can readily see the Profit score of 8 percent on the chart.

We can also easily do the math in our heads and that's why I prefer to use USD redeemed value per 1000 points rather than cents per point, unlike some travel bloggers.

POINT BUSTER

We multiply the Earn Rate score by our Returns score and then divide by 10. In this case, 4 multiplied by 20, then divided by 10, to arrive at 8 percent. If achieved in a real-world application, that simply means that spending USD400 earning points would release USD32 in redeemed value.

We can use the Profit score table to check the potential Profit scores of any combination of Earn Rate and Returns and for any airline loyalty program.

Let's apply the concept to compare a 5 percent cash back credit card to one that earns points. I've added a line joining combinations of Earn Rate and Returns delivering a Profit score of 5 percent (see Figure 29).

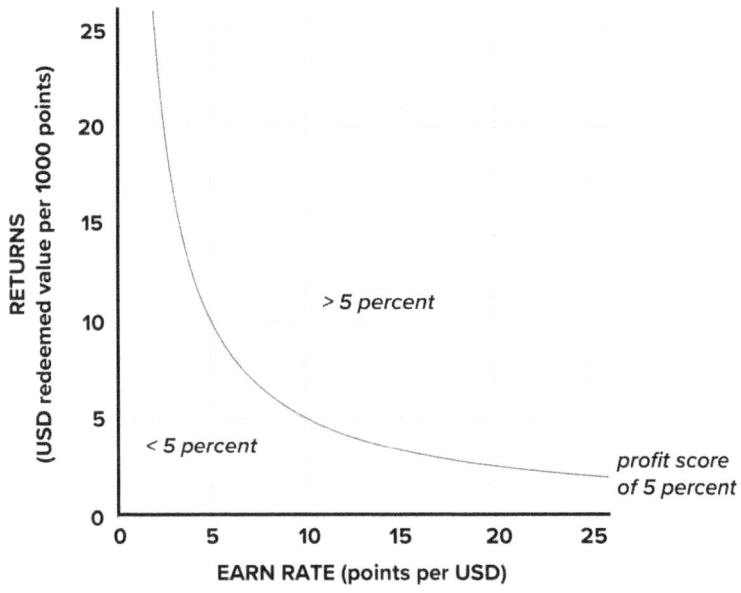

Figure 29: The curve for a Profit score of 5 percent

STRATEGY

Assuming that we accept redeemed value rather than cash back and ignore any transaction and other card fees, we outperform the cash-back credit card given any combination of Earn Rate and Returns to the right of the curve.

Thus, when earning points at 3 points per USD, we need to achieve Returns greater than about USD17 redeemed value per 1000 points to outperform the cash back credit card.

Now let's set a target for our Profit score. Let's assume that to be the equivalent of a half price discount in a shop, thus a Profit score of 100 percent, since the redeemed value released is the same as the cash spent.

For that, we need to look at greater variation in Earn Rate and Returns. I extended the table up to 100 points per USD for Earn Rate and USD100 redeemed value per 1000 points for Returns. (see Figure 30).

profit score (%)

RETURNS (USD redeemed value per 1000 points)	10	20	30	40	50	60	70	80	90	100
100										100 200 300 400 500 600 700 800 900 1000

100	100	200	300	400	500	600	700	800	900	1000
90	90	180	270	360	450	540	630	720	810	900
80	80	160	240	320	400	480	560	640	720	800
70	70	140	210	280	350	420	490	560	630	700
60	60	120	180	240	300	360	420	480	540	600
50	50	100	150	200	250	300	350	400	450	500
40	40	80	120	160	200	240	280	320	360	400
30	30	60	90	120	150	180	210	240	270	300
20	20	40	60	80	100	120	140	160	180	200
10	10	20	30	40	50	60	70	80	90	100
	10	20	30	40	50	60	70	80	90	100

EARN RATE (points per USD)

Figure 30: Widely different Profit scores are possible

The axes step up in intervals of ten units, because the full table would be too big to fit in this book. Now the highest Profit score in the table is 1000 percent, achieved through a combination of an Earn Rate of 100 points per USD and Returns of USD100 redeemed value per 1000 points.

If ever achieved, that reward would deliver an extremely rare ten times more in redeemed value than the cash spent on stuff earning points in the first place.

Our potential Profit scores will lie between zero, when we don't even redeem our points, up to the theoretical maximum. There are any number of theoretically possible combinations in between.

For example, we can attain a Profit score of 60 percent, when earning points at 20 points per USD, and then redeeming them for a reward offering USD30 redeemed value per 1000 points.

Now because we earn our points before redeeming them, Our Earn Rate limits our potential Profit scores, or in practical terms, what part of the table is relevant.

When earning 10 points per USD for a certain transaction, that Earn Rate becomes locked in. All of the area of the table to the right of the column for the value of 10 on the horizontal axis becomes irrelevant. Only a small part of the table is in play. The bad news is that this puts a limit on our Profit score. The good news is that by improving our Earn Rate, ever more of the table comes into play.

A quick look at the numbers in the table also shows that most Profit scores are much lower that the theoretical maximum score. In short, most combinations of Earn Rate and Returns deliver relatively low Profit scores.

Basically, we need to aim to improve our Earn Rate ***and*** Returns to boost our Profit score. For example, if we can step up our Earn Rate from 10 to 20 points per USD, by stacking our earning streams for the same transaction, and our Returns from USD10 to USD20 redeemed value per 1000 points, by choosing a more valuable redemption, that would quadruple our Profit score from 10 to 40 percent.

Obviously, we can pick whatever Profit score target that we want. Let's add the curve for our nominated Profit score of 100 percent (see Figure 31).

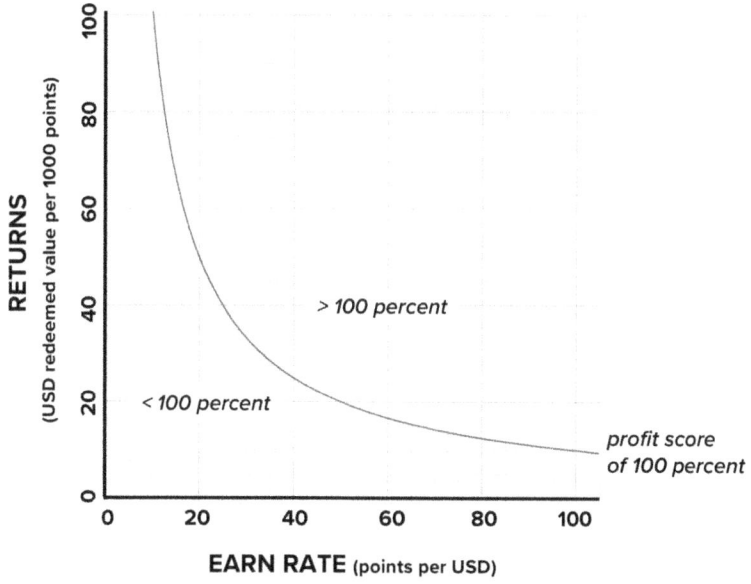

Figure 31: The curve for a Profit score of 100 percent

Now we can see which combinations underperform and which exceed that target, since they are respectively below or above the curve.

Taking my recent grocery shop Earn Rate of 15 points per USD, I need to target a redemption offering at least USD67 points per USD to achieve a Profit score of 100 percent.

On my upcoming reward redemption, Cairns to Frankfurt in Singapore Airlines business class using Virgin Velocity points, I'll fall just short with a Profit score of 90 percent.

But I'll still accrue USD90 of redeemed value for every USD100 spent on groceries, whilst meeting my travel goal and without the additional opportunity cost of alternative routing options.

The final step in the evolution of our Profit score tables is to visualize how they can apply to any airline loyalty program of choice. For that we can simply set the range of values for both Earn Rate and Returns on their respective axes, to scope the maximum potential variation in any given program.

Examples: I was able to travel from Australia to French Polynesia, by redeeming Qantas Frequent flyer points for business class flights on Qantas and Air Tahiti Nui.

I targeted a relatively very fast Earn Rate of about 70 points per USD by buying Qantas Wine. And then I selected relatively rich Returns of about USD25 redeemed value per 1000 points, about 7 times higher than the base redeemed value, if I'd redeemed points for a gift voucher.

Since the Award Seats were available and the points redeemed, the theoretical Profit score was the same as the actual Pay-off, at 70 times 25 divided 10, thus 175 percent.

Whereas I could have theoretically found rewards offering richer Returns, I met my travel goals and still enjoyed USD175 of redeemed value for every USD100 of cash spend.

STRATEGY

Strategy: let's explore four strategies, which impact Profit. I've simply defined these by whether a player earns their points fast or slow, and by whether they redeem their flyer points for rewards of relatively richer or poorer Returns (see Figure 32).

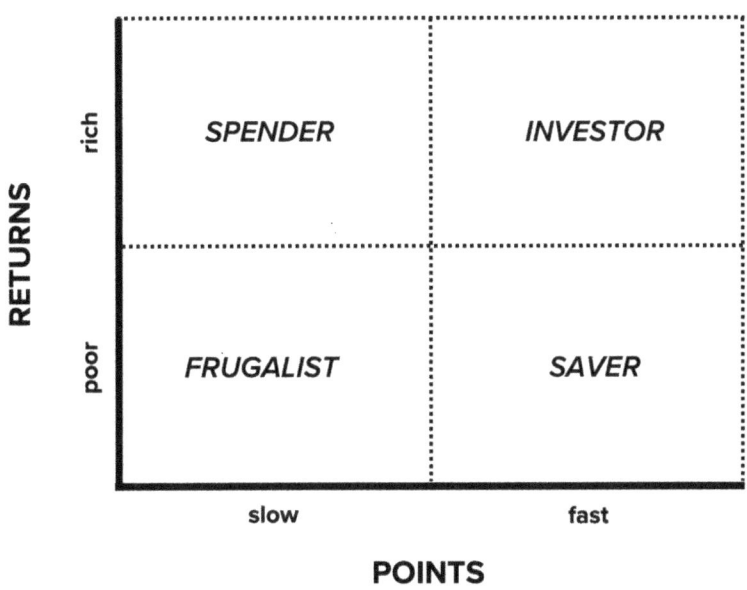

Figure 32: Strategies impacting PROFIT

Strategy **Frugalist** is to save cash at the time of purchase. This strategy requires that the player aims to spend less at the till, regardless of their flyer point earn.

The player doesn't bother to seek out higher Earn Rates and thereby earns their flyer points slowly, because their focus is to shop around for the best cash deal. They accrue low point totals, so can only redeem their points for a goal reward of relatively poor redeemed value.

One example is when a shopper earns points, but puts no effort into chasing down opportunities to earn them above the base Earn Rate. Another example is when a player travels on cheap economy-coach airfares, which attract either zero or low point earn.

The upside of strategy Frugalist is that the player doesn't need to expend much effort. They can focus on finding the cheapest cash deals at the time of purchase to stretch their cash spend. They accrue enough points for a domestic economy flight or a low-value gift voucher with little risk.

The downside is that the player bypasses richer reward otherwise attainable through their everyday spend by seeking relatively higher Earn Rates and Returns. They tend to experience relatively poor Returns because they are restricted by their relatively low total points, which limits their choice of reward.

Strategy **Spender** is to leverage substantive cash flow to amass lots of points. This strategy requires a player to accrue many points, albeit through transactions that can typically have low Earn Rates. They can still accrue ample points to drive a flexible portfolio and thereby access available Target Rewards of relatively rich Returns.

An example is when a business owner earns flyer points through their business cash flow. They have a business credit card, and purchase business related products and services from airline loyalty program partners.

They make payments via a third-party financial platform offering flyer point earn and credit card point earn, such as Bluechain in the UK, and Yak Pay in Australia, to cite a couple of examples without favor.

The upside of strategy Spender is that a player can amass substantive volumes of flyer points, even in the millions per year. They can then transfer them into their personal program account to be redeemed to satisfy their personal travel goals.

The downside is that the player is potentially missing out on greater Profit and thereby higher Pay-offs given target Reward availability, unless they take advantage of available opportunities to earn their points faster.

Strategy **Saver** is to stretch a nominated travel budget by redeeming points instead of paying cash for airfares. This strategy requires that the player is adept at taking advantage of relatively higher point earn and accruing points fast.

But then they risk redeeming those points at relatively poor redeemed values, because they target cash savings rather than bang for buck, when choosing their rewards.

An example is when a frequent traveler and everyday spender has a limited travel budget. Imagine a family with a couple of children. Their goal is to manage a travel budget for a family vacation. Their preference is to redeem their flyer points for multiple seats on the same flight.

But their points total has to accommodate multiple passengers. Furthermore, their opportunity to redeem for premium cabins is potentially limited by reward seat availability, since multiple reward seats in business and first class are less likely to be released on the same flight than just one or two.

Their redemption goal thereby targets economy-coach, which in turn tends to offer relatively less redeemed value for their points.

The upside of strategy Saver is the player can perceive a cash saving equal to the retail airfare or their nominated budget, when they don't need to purchase those flights redeemed with flyer points. The player can then redirect that part of their travel budget towards other expenses, such as food, entertainment, or accommodation.

The downside is that although the player manages to stretch their budget, they risk receiving less bang for buck for their flyer points and original spend earning those points.

Finally, strategy **Investor** is to unleash the most bang for buck for the original everyday cash spend that earns points. This strategy requires that the player is highly adept at the flyer point game. They seek out both relatively fast point Earn Rates and higher Returns. They appreciate that opportunities to do both accelerate their Profit score and thereby their Payoff given Target Reward availability.

One example is when a shopper methodically tracks down opportunities to earn their points and also to elevate their Earn Rates for the full scope of their everyday spend, be that on airfares, travel, or any other personal, household, or business expenditure.

They harness relevant point earn bonuses, transfer bonuses, deploy credit cards offering sign up and retention bonuses, onboard their family members and consolidate their points totals, and so forth.

They do the math and set their point valuation bar high before making reward redemptions to target more redeemed value relative to their original cash spend, whilst also satisfying their personal travel goals.

STRATEGY

Another example is when a very frequent traveller has business or first-class airfares paid by their employer and also earns points fast through their personal and household spend.

They extend the scope of their opportunity to earn points and they search out relatively high point earn. They are familiar with the benefits of elite travel and thereby prefer to redeem their points for business or first-class Target Rewards.

The upside of strategy Investor is the player can accelerate their Profit score by combining both a higher Earn Rate with richer Returns. Given Target Reward seat availability, they can access the upper end of Pay-offs attainable in the flyer point game and enjoy travel rich reward.

The downside is that the player needs to be sufficiently skilled and up-to-date to track down both relatively higher Earn Rates and relatively higher Returns. This requires continued commitment and effort.

They also need to find the balance between seeking to optimize redeemed value for their points and satisfying their personal travel goals.

Take outs: strategy Investor is theoretically the optimal strategy to boost higher Profit. In practice, we simply combine action power pack PROPEL to earn points faster with action power pack ENRICH to redeem more value per point.

Value is generated by how easily that we can earn our points *and* how much redeemed value that those points deliver. It's the variation in both that can accelerate Profit.

Since we earn our points before we can redeem them, it's the Earn Rate that ultimately limits the Profit score. Points earned at relatively low Earn Rates can never deliver greater Profit scores than points earned at relatively high Earn Rates.

Of course, in real-life scenarios, players earn their points at all sorts of different rates, and they redeem their points for all sorts of rewards delivering widely differing redeemed values. They experience a whole range of Pay-offs depending upon their specific earn and redemption transactions.

How can we improve upon the suboptimal strategies of Frugalist, Spender, and Saver?

Strategy Frugalist earns points slowly and is redeemed value poor. We can address that by combining the actions in power pack PROPEL to earn points faster with those in power pack ENRICH to redeem more value per point.

Strategy Spender earns points slowly. We can apply action power pack PROPEL to earn points faster. Finally, strategy Saver is redeemed value poor. We can apply action power pack ENRICH to redeem more value per point.

In reality, the definitions and application of the four strategies are fluid. In practice, any player can adopt any one at any time. Thus, we'll face situations in which we earn our points slowly rather than leave them behind. Similarly, we might redeem our points for relatively lower redeemed value than preferable, because of a compelling personal need or want, such as stretching a travel budget for a vacation.

Of course, we're talking theoretical Profit scores. We also need to outsmart the interplay between value and availability of our Target Rewards to unlock our Pay-off.

Spoiler alert – that's why there's a hidden trap in our path, that we're about to meet, and learn how to outwit.

JUST LIVE IT: boost higher Profit

PAY-OFF

In the flyer point game, the greater our Pay-off the more travel rich reward that we can enjoy for our everyday spend. We unleash more bang for buck. It's finally time to fuse all of our gameplay together to generate a winning Pay-off.

The POINT BUSTER has four overlapping circles. There's only one part left to reveal, namely, the overlaps of all four circles right in the middle. That core is where all of the parts come together to determine our Pay-off (see Figure 33).

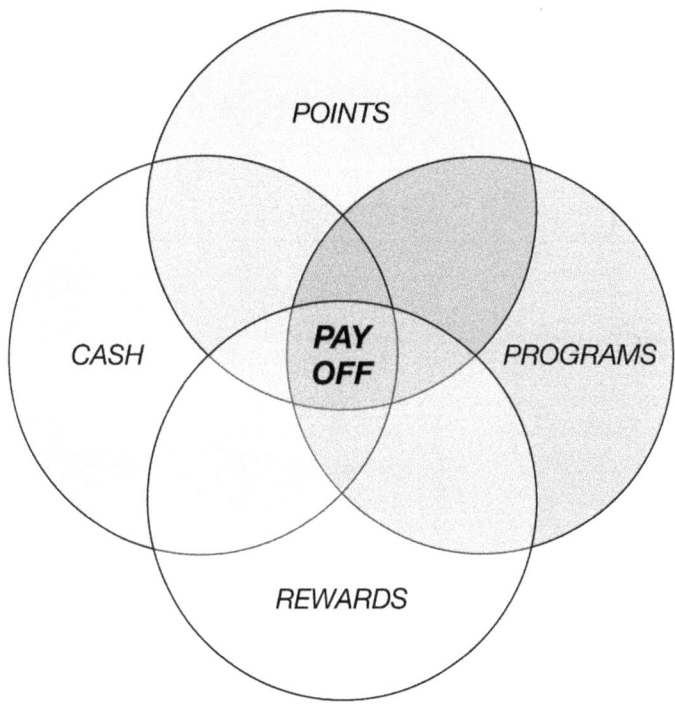

Figure 33: Pay-off depends upon all of the parts

POINT BUSTER

Pay-offs vary greatly. I typically achieve scores in the range of 50 to 100 percent. The maximum, excluding obvious "mistake" offers, was an utterly exceptional 3000 percent. It was based upon a SIM card promotion with an Earn Rate of 300 points per USD and first-class reward seats with Returns of about USD100 redeemed value per 1000 points.

In reality players experience a broad range of Pay-offs. To achieve the relatively higher scores, we need **all** of our four action power packs and our four boosters in play. This is because we're pitted against a system in which one factor can impact another. Let's look at just at some of the interactions relating to total points (see Figure 34).

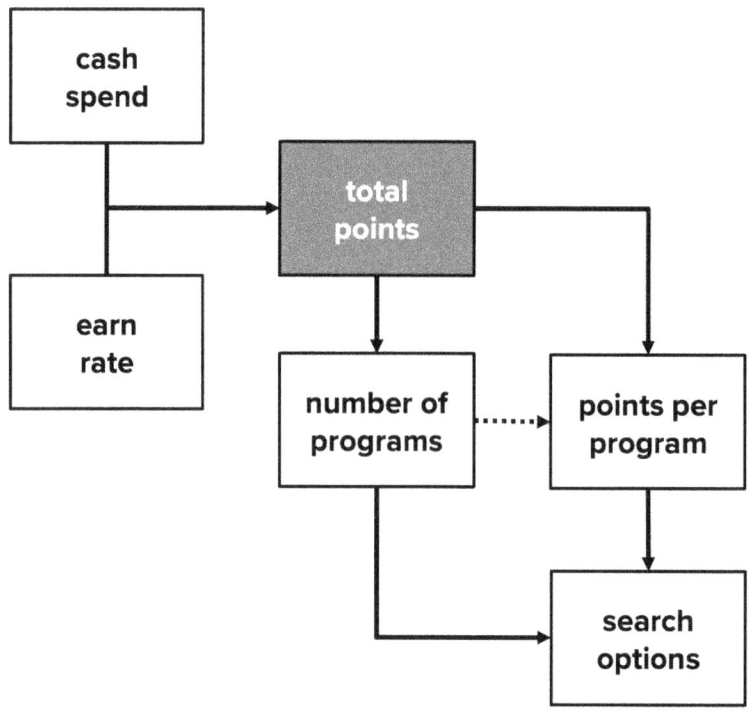

Figure 34: Impacts of total points (dashed arrows are negative)

Our points total depends upon both cash spend and Earn Rate. In turn, our capacity to diversify our program portfolio depends upon our total number of points. And then the number of our reward search Options depends upon our number of programs and points per program.

But there is also a negative feedback loop. Adding programs reduces our average points per program for a given total number of points. We need to balance total points, programs, points per program, and search Options.

Because everything is interconnected, there is a four-way trap revealed in the POINT BUSTER as those areas where three, but not all four, circles overlap (see Figure 35).

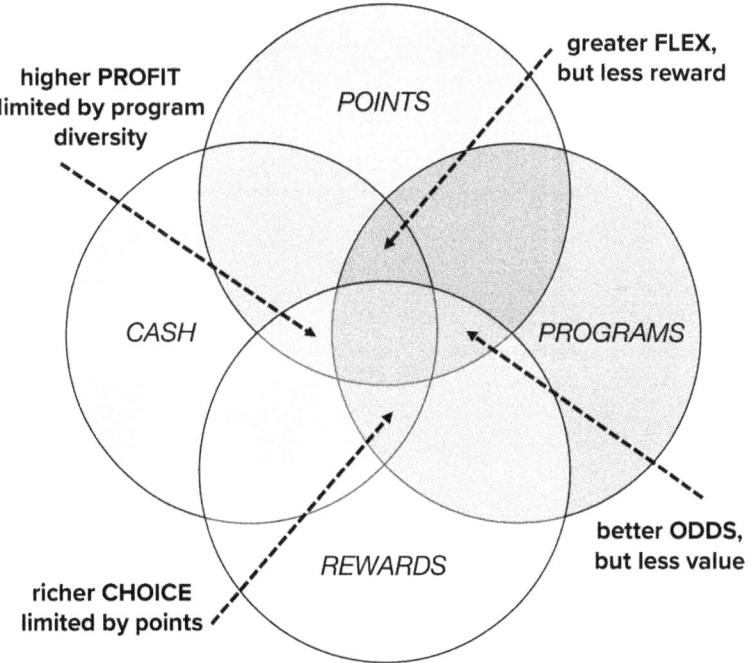

Figure 35: There is a four-way trap

POINT BUSTER

Basically, a low points total can limit richer Choice. Poor program diversity can limit higher Profit. Failing to turn over rewards can generate greater Flex, but less reward. Ignoring cash when measuring our gameplay can direct us towards better Odds of success, but lower redeemed value and thereby less bang for buck. Let's explore how to outsmart each part of this hidden four-way trap.

JUST LIVE IT: outsmart the system

(Chao Phraya River from The Peninsula Bangkok)

WIN BY MILES

Juice

Having sufficient points is critical to our gameplay. But we can be points poor and sit outside the circle of points in the POINT BUSTER. It's time to juice up and target more points. Otherwise, we can be restricted to redeeming rewards, that require lesser numbers of points.

Furthermore, Target Rewards offering relatively higher redeemed value, such as business and first-class reward seats, tend to require more points. Having insufficient points potentially limits the redeemed value of our reward. This restricts our richer Choice (see Figure 36).

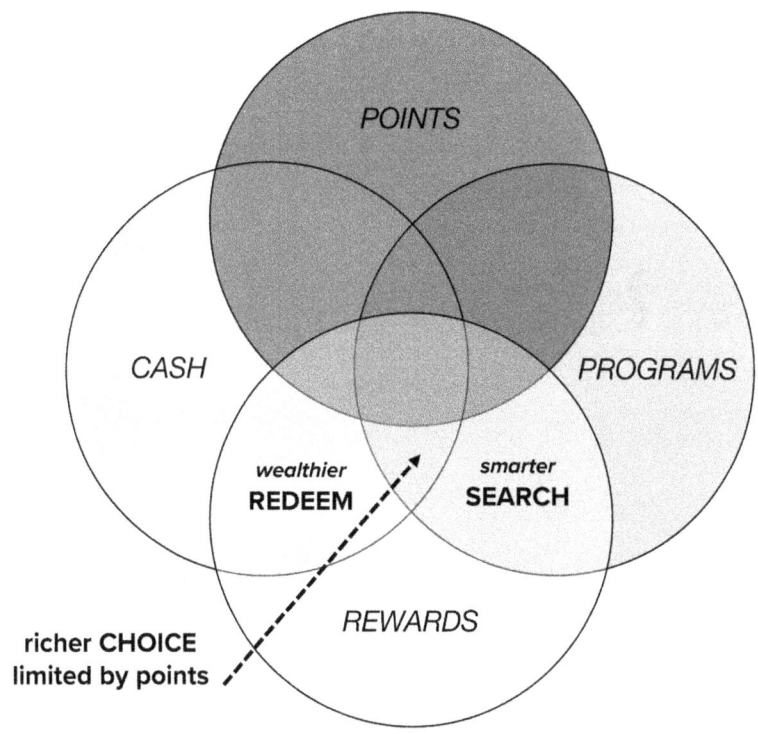

Figure 36: Points limit richer CHOICE

Having insufficient points also curbs our capacity to diversify our points portfolio to outwit the limited availability of our Target Rewards, whilst harnessing the specific strengths and sweet spots of any given airline loyalty program. That in turn also impacts our richer Choice.

The answer is simple, to direct more of our everyday spend to earn points and to earn points at a higher Earn Rate for that spend. The ideal is to target both.

We can achieve that by applying the actions in power pack PROPEL for a faster earn. But our success depends upon the available opportunities to earn points offered by those programs in our portfolio.

Now for the good news and bad news. The good news is that Earn Rates can vary widely. Relatively high Earn Rates can juice up our points faster.

The bad news is that relatively higher Earn Rates are less accessible than relatively lower Earn Rates. They are harder to find. There's no free lunch. Effort is needed take advantage of the opportunities that they present.

Average: let's consider some data from the *"Qantas Annual Report 2024"*. Some 16.4 million then members of Qantas Frequent Flyer earned 202 billion points in the 2024 financial year.

Of course, we don't know how many members have been inactive in the 12-month period, thereby accruing zero points. But we can still easily calculate an estimate for the average number of points earned by all members, active in the year or not, by dividing 202 billion by 16.4 million.

That's very roughly 12,500 points per member per year. If 12,500 is the approximate average total points earned over a year by a member, then it's clearly not going to do much for our goal of travel rich rewards. That's in the ballpark of only enough points for a short one-way economy class redemption or a USD35 gift card.

Ideally, a winning points per year target could be at least up to hundred times or even more than that. We simply can't afford to think in terms of being average, rather aim to perform well ahead of the bell curve.

When I look at my own points earning history several things are immediately striking. Most point earning transactions are routine, but generate relatively few points. There is an ongoing steady accrual of flyer points from certain point earning opportunities, such as my weekly grocery shopping and credit card spend plodding along in the background. That's fine because we don't want to bypass opportunities to accrue our points.

But the vast majority of my points have been earned through less predictable opportunities. These are occasional and have included a promotion for my small business to buy fuel, SIM card subscriptions, and unusually high bonuses on retail purchases.

There's a pattern in which lower Earn Rates pair with more predictable opportunities that generate relatively few points. At the other end of the scale, there are less predictable opportunities coupled with higher Earn Rates, which yield relatively huge numbers of points. Let's explore the idea using risk analysis.

POINT BUSTER

Risk: there are three parts to the concept of risk, namely, an event, the probability that it occurs, and its potential impact. In risk analysis, we seek to avoid or mitigate risky events.

Control of risk can be factored into our gameplay in the flyer point game. One risk that can have immediate and downstream impacts on key aspects of our gameplay is missing an opportunity to accrue our points and to do that faster.

We can be so focused on something to be entirely blind to what's staring us in the face. To prove it, researchers Christopher Chabris and Daniel Simons, created a selective attention test. Viewers watch a video of a group of moving people and count how many times a ball is passed between them. Spoiler alert - viewers tend not to notice somebody in a gorilla suit walking through the field of play.

We can become distracted in the flyer point game by putting our focus on our saved points and wanting to know how much they are worth, the availability of reward seats, and the best redemption opportunities. But none of these come into play until ***after*** earning our points.

We can also become fixated on our comfortable and familiar methods to earn points, such as credit card sign up bonuses and ongoing earn. But other game-changing opportunities can also be staring us in the face. These can expand our scope to earn points.

For example, we can easily miss an amazing opportunity to earn points that crops up in an airline loyalty program outside of our field of view because that program is not part of our regular portfolio of programs and thereby not on our radar.

PAY-OFF

Identifying opportunity can require the effort to expand our horizons and update ourselves by regularly checking the headlines of our preferred travel blogs. There are extensive additional avenues to earn our points, we just have to be able to see that gorilla walking across our field of view. One totally unexpected recent promotion by SAS EuroBonus offered a bonus of one million points for members, who earned or redeemed points flying on 15 SkyTeam partners airlines.

Opportunity: we can invert the concept of negative risk to focus on positive risk, namely, opportunity. Let's consider an event, its probability and its impact, but now seek to identify opportunity with the goal of harnessing its positive impact. Let's apply that to our goal to accelerate our point earn and compare the probability, effort, and impact of relatively different Earn Rates (see Figure 37).

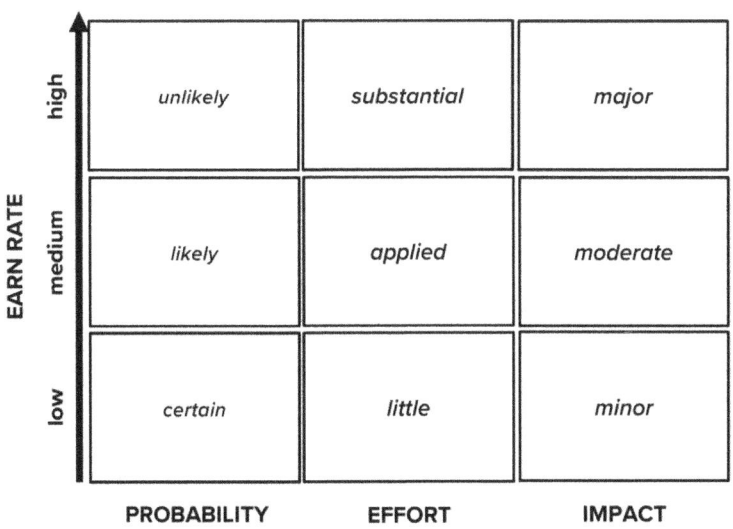

Figure 37: We can seek opportunities for higher Earn Rates

POINT BUSTER

We're certain to earn some points at low Earn Rates when purchasing from any program partner or paying with a point-earning credit card.

These transactions take little effort, but only have relatively minor impact. Accruing 80,000 points in one year requires a spend of USD20,000 at an average overall Earn Rate of 4 points per USD. At low Earn Rates, the volume of our spend directed at earning points limits or liberates our performance.

Some players of the flyer point game ***can*** earn vast numbers of points through their business spend at relatively low Earn Rates. The sheer volume of cash flow drives a tidy accrual of points. That's great. But there's also the potential to accrue points through individual everyday cash spend at greatly varying Earn Rates

Let's step it up to consider medium Earn Rates. These are likely, take some effort and have a moderate impact. Now a spend of USD20,000 annually, at say, an average Earn Rate of 15 points per USD, can accrue 300,000 points per year. At medium Earn Rates, our own level of effort limits or liberates our performance.

Let's talk effort. The flyer point game is like any other, when starting out we need to learn how to move the pieces and keep the score. This takes time and requires dedication.

Even when we're up and running, there's always something new, since the flyer point universe is dynamic and always changing. We need to keep up to date by regularly checking our favorite travel blogs for relevant news and then develop our skills, including how to earn our points faster. In short, there's a hidden cost.

Luckily, increased effort can have a significant impact. Small changes in actions and approach can greatly improve what we can enjoy as our reward. And, ultimately, earning sufficient points has many downstream impacts in the flyer point game, that affect our Pay-off.

Stepping it up again, high Earn Rates are unlikely to occur, but still do so often enough that a smart player prepared to put in substantial effort will be ready to harness the opportunity. The potential impact is major.

A spend of USD20,000 at 50 points per USD sets us up to crack the one million points per year league. Assuming commitment to the game, at high Earn Rates, the probability of opportunity limits or liberates our performance.

In summary, it's easy to overlook that probability plays a part when we earn our points as well as when we seek Target Rewards of limited availability. Opportunities to earn points at modest Earn Rates are common, whereas those with relatively higher Earn Rates are relatively rare. We can aim to harness opportunities presenting those higher Earn Rates.

Beyond the bell curve: now let's step it up even one more level and beyond the boundaries of our simple opportunity matrix. Some events of huge impact wouldn't even make a risk or opportunity matrix because they are perceived as far too rare to feature in conventional thinking.

Occasionally there are very unpredictable high impact events in the flyer point game. The SAS EuroBonus challenge cited above would potentially return an Earn Rate of 100 points per USD given an opportunity cost of USD10,000 or 200 points per USD given an opportunity cost of USD5000, in addition to the swag of one million bonus points.

That example would potentially break our guiding principle of earning our points from everyday spend. We're effectively buying points, unless already committed to purchase the qualifying flights.

At such unusually huge Earn Rates, our own sass limits or liberates our performance with game-changing impact. Players can miss out, if they're distracted or unaware of such extraordinary opportunities. Such events have the potential to revolutionize our engagement in the flyer point game.

Take outs: our performance in the flyer point game is ultimately determined by our capacity to earn and restock our points.

It's typically easy to accrue points at low Earn Rates, since these are commonly accessible. But unless we're spending big cash, that won't accrue points quickly.

We'll find relatively higher Earn Rates, although tracking these down can take time and effort. But the potential positive impact is that much greater for the same cash spend.

There will also be very occasional opportunities to harness relatively huge Earn Rates. These can present a route to amass vast numbers of points.

In short, being limited or liberated in our gameplay can depend upon how well that we can recognize and respond to the various opportunities to accrue our flyer points.

JUST LIVE IT: hunt plentiful points

PAY-OFF

(Sagrada Família, Barcelona)

DREAM TO REALITY

POINT BUSTER

Status

Status sounds great. It offers bounty like access to lounges, priority check in, upgrades, and recognition as an elite member. But there's a catch. Status can distract us from diversifying our gameplay across multiple airline loyalty programs. We can be programs poor and sit outside the circle of programs in the POINT BUSTER. And that can restrict our opportunities to earn and redeem our points.

We can miss out on more efficient ways to manage our points portfolio to unleash value from our points. Status can thereby potentially limit higher Profit (see Figure 38).

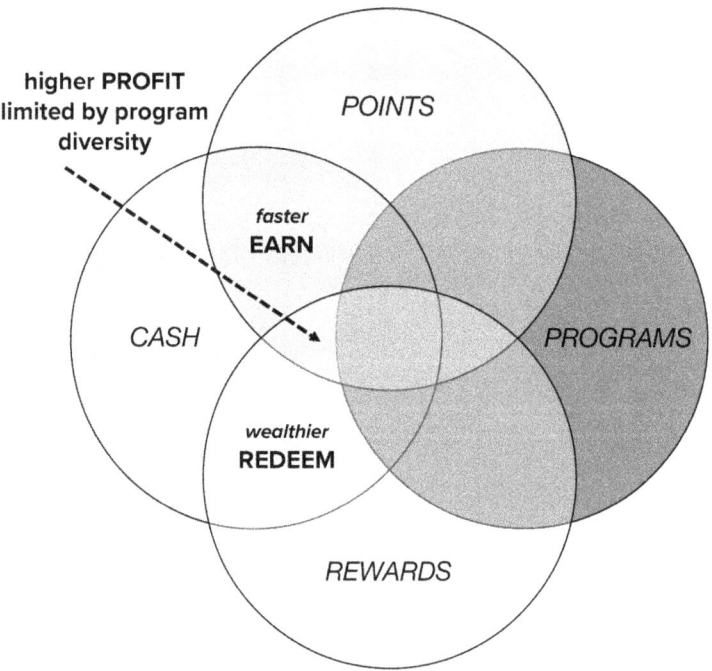

Figure 38: Program diversity limits higher PROFIT

For years, I focused on status and let the points look after themselves. But the bubble can eventually burst if the value, which we perceive, exceeds the actual value delivered.

My primary goal shifted to unleashing the power of my flyer points. I decided to focus on the points and let the status look after itself. But that's just me, so let's take an objective look at the upsides and downsides of status and then evaluate whether it works for us individually.

Status tiers: each airline loyalty program is a little different, so let's imagine a typified model offered by our hypothetical Jet Zest Airlines Loyalty Program. Our status is assigned by tier level according to how much business we bring each year to the program's parent airline and airline partners. There are four status tiers with precious sounding names, Osmium, Palladium, Iridium, and Rhodium (see Figure 39).

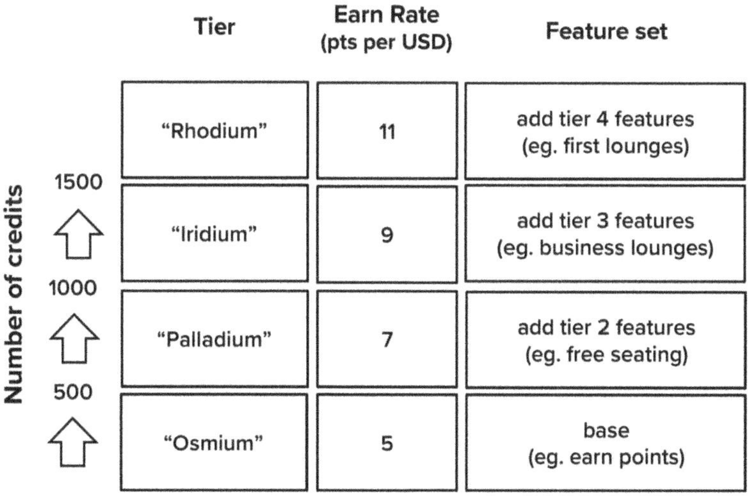

Tier	Earn Rate (pts per USD)	Feature set
"Rhodium"	11	add tier 4 features (eg. first lounges)
"Iridium"	9	add tier 3 features (eg. business lounges)
"Palladium"	7	add tier 2 features (eg. free seating)
"Osmium"	5	base (eg. earn points)

Number of credits: 500, 1000, 1500

Figure 39: Status tiers of the Jet Zest Loyalty Program

POINT BUSTER

Members join the program at the entry level Osmium tier and step up the tiers. The status tiers offer opportunity to benefit from increasing Earn Rates for airline spend and various tier features. It's important for the airline to lock in the higher spenders of airfares and entice them with the trappings of status, so the top status tiers are described as elite. Then the most loyal members can feel that extra bit special.

There are several ways to assign status tiers in the airline loyalty universe, varying from distance flown, sectors flown, cash spend, and so forth. Some programs allocate status credits and publish how many we can earn for a given flight sector, cabin class, fare type and whether buying an airfare and flying with the parent airline, or one of its alliance or other partner airlines.

In our hypothetical program, there's a 12-month period to accrue the status credits cycling from when members first joined the program. Each year, the status credit total resets to zero forcing members to accrue their credits all over again. Other programs use a calendar year.

The achieved status tier is assigned for just one year before being reviewed. In other programs the achieved status tier lasts for the rest of the year in which it was attained and through the following year.

Fewer status credits are needed to requalify for a given status tier in subsequent membership periods, for example, in our hypothetical program 1250 credits to requalify for top tier compared with 1500 for the initial qualification target.

Some program members map the various status tier feature sets to their needs and wants and target one status tier below the top tier. This becomes their status tier sweet spot.

Airline loyalty programs can offer status matches to members of other programs. Those with status can thereby diversify their engagement with multiple programs, whilst maintaining status in more than one.

Members can eventually attain lifetime status tier recognition afforded by some airline loyalty programs, thereby, ironically a ticket off the hamster wheel of continually having to retain their status tier every year.

Some players go on mileage or status runs to ensure that they reach their annual target to attain or maintain a certain status tier. Travel blogs can share the hacks of the day to reach elite status tiers more efficiently.

These can include how to fly the most distance for the least cost for those programs with mileage-based status accrual and the most flights for the least cost for those programs with sector-based accrual. Members of programs with status credits accrual can share how to earn the most status credits for the least cost.

The British Airways Club and Virgin Australia Velocity have recently joined those programs, which directly or indirectly relate status tier recognition to cash spend. This effectively targets high spenders and restricts the ability of members to use shortcuts to qualify for higher status tiers.

Some programs run promotions to entice airfare spend, for example, the double status credit offers of Qantas Airways Qantas Frequent Flyer and Virgin Australia Velocity.

Impacts of status: there's ample detailed information on status on travel blogs. We'll adopt an objective approach to unpack the upsides and downsides. I've drawn a simple map summarizing positive and negative impacts (see Figure 40).

POINT BUSTER

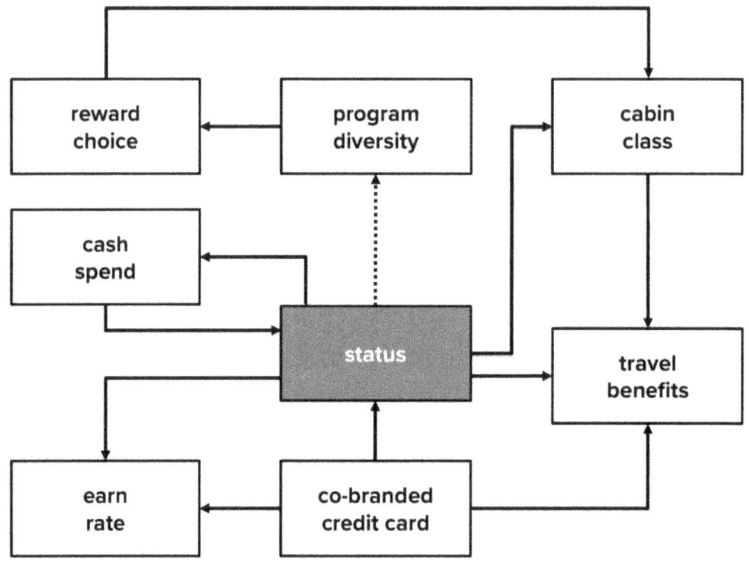

Figure 40: Positive and negative (dashed line) impacts of status

Cash spend: our cash spend ***positively*** impacts our level of status. Status is just another part of loyalty marketing. It's just part of a business designed to scoop up ever more coin. It always comes back to the cash. Basically, the more spend, the higher our status tier.

Whether status tiers are assessed by cash spend or the number of flight sectors, distance, and so forth, it all comes down to measuring the extent of our loyal cash spend and locking in our continued business.

Our hypothetical program quite simply allocates one status credit for every USD5 spent buying airfares and traveling on partner airlines.

To reach the top status tier of Rhodium a member needs to spend USD7500 to accrue the associated target of 1500 status credits.

By return, status ***positively*** impacts our cash spend. Practically speaking that just means that we are encouraged to spend more.

Research published in *"Marketing Science"* by Yeshim Orhun and co-authors concludes that members can be willing to pay higher prices for airfares to satisfy their desire to attain and maintain elite status, especially when employers pick up the tab. We can get caught in the loop of cash spend promoting status and status encouraging cash spend.

Co-branded credit card: a co-branded credit card can have a ***positive*** impact on status. Our hypothetical program includes spend on the Jet Zest Airlines co-branded credit card when assessing status tier.

Programs offering such a facility include American Airlines AAdvantage, Delta Air Lines SkyMiles, Qatar Airways Privilege Club, and United Airlines MileagePlus. There is an HSBC Star Alliance Credit Card in Australia offering gold status, if spend targets are reached.

The Jet Zest Airlines co-branded credit card has a ***positive*** impact on Earn Rate. Our hypothetical program has a typical card sign-up bonus of 60,000 points for a USD4000 spend in the first three months, thereby delivering 15 points per USD during that period.

Additionally, the card offers Earnings of 3 points per USD for parent airline purchases, 2 points per USD for dining and travel and 1 point per USD for other purchases. Points can be earned making any transaction using the card.

The Jet Zest Airlines hypothetical co-branded credit card also has a ***positive*** impact on travel benefits by offering lounge access. Similarly, certain American Express personal and business cards offer access to Delta Sky Club when traveling on a same-day ticket, to cite just one example.

Co-branded credit cards can also offer a range of other features, such as discounted rewards and first bag checked free and so forth. These can be of value according to the needs and wants of individual members.

Earn rates: our status tier level can have a ***positive*** impact on Earn Rate when purchasing our airfares, since Earn Rate steps up with higher status tier. Those extra points can appear attractive, especially if our travel is paid for by our employer.

But what's the catch? We can easily see the total points earned by flying within a given airline loyalty program by simply looking at our online activity statements. But the ***extra*** points earned is not immediately obvious without doing the math.

So, let's see how many extra points accrue in our hypothetical program as an annual spend increasing from zero to USD10,000 elevates our status tier.

In our hypothetical program, we only accrue extra points through status given a spend of USD2500 triggering a step up from Osmium to Palladium. Thereafter we earn more extra points as we step up the status tiers. Spending USD10,000, accrues a total of 30,000 extra points. By then, the extra Earn Rate is 30,000 divided by 10,000, thus 3 points per USD (see Figure 41).

STARTING FROM STATUS TIER ONE (USD10k spend)

Tier	Earn Rate (pts per USD)	Spend range	Extra points
Status Tier Four "Rhodium"	+6	USD7500 to USD10,000	15,000 (6 x 2500)
Status Tier Three "Iridium"	+4	USD5000 to USD7500	10,000 (4 x 2500)
Status Tier Two "Palladium"	+2	USD2500 to USD5000	5,000 (2 x 2500)
Status Tier One "Osmium"	+0	up to USD2500	0 (0 x 2500)
			Total 30,000

Figure 41: Extra points earned by status tier

The extra Earn Rate trends upwards with more spend, but never exceeds 6 points per USD, the maximum defined for the top status tier in this model and that applicable to those members, who retain the top status tier.

For perspective, let's put that in terms of the impact on our potential Profit score. We can calculate that by multiplying the extra Earn Rate by our Returns and divide by 10.

In our hypothetical program the maximum extra Earn Rate is 6 points per USD, which means that for every step up of USD5 redeemed value per 1000 points in our Returns, our Profit score would improve by 6 times 5 divide by 10, thus 3 percent. We'd need to rework the math for any given program and decide for ourselves, if that's worthwhile.

POINT BUSTER

Travel benefits: our status tier level can have a ***positive*** impact on the travel benefits enjoyed as higher tiers offer ever more enticing features that we might personally value (see Figure 42).

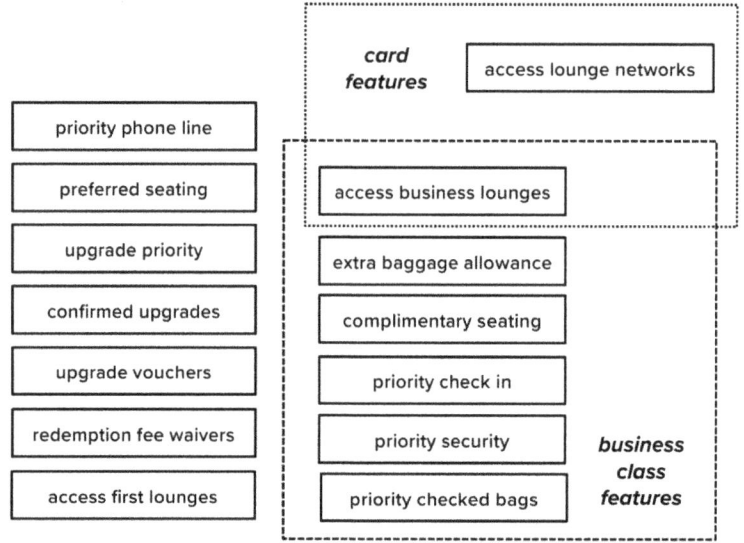

Figure 42: Features of the top status tier for Jet Zest Airlines

These can include a priority phone line, upgrade priority, priority check-in, security lines and boarding, to preferred and complimentary seating, to access to the parent and program partner airlines' business and first-class lounges, depending upon the program.

Incidentally, access to airline lounges can be excluded when traveling on domestic flights in the USA for members of US-based airline loyalty programs. It can be best to check. Partner programs of non-US airlines can sometimes include such access as part of a status tier feature set.

Cabin class: status tier level can have a ***positive*** impact on cabin class of travel. Some programs bestow upgrade certificates for higher status. But using them can depend upon the availability of upgrades. Available upgrade seats can also be allocated based upon where we sit in the hierarchy, which can typically be our status tier.

Program diversity: if status serves its intended goal of locking in our airline business, status can have a ***negative*** impact on program diversity, our engagement over multiple airline loyalty programs.

This can divert our attention away from the opportunity to harness the individual strengths and sweet spots of other programs and thereby how efficiently we can use our flyer points once redeemed given our travel goals.

It can also be prudent to belong to those airline loyalty programs that tend to release more rewards seats, especially those in business and first class, to their own members.

Reward Choice: because status can detract from program diversity, it can undermine the downstream positive impacts of program diversity. Status can ***negatively*** impact our reward choice. This can be significant when searching out Target Rewards with limited availability. We simply have lesser Odds of success.

Because status undermines program diversity and thereby reward choice, it indirectly ***negatively*** impacts our scope to access Target Rewards of relatively higher redeemed value, including those in premium cabin classes.

POINT BUSTER

Alternatives: paid airfares and Target Rewards in premium cabin classes give us an alternate route to many of the tier features of status itself. Let's divide up the feature set for the top tier of our hypothetical Jet Zest Airlines loyalty program (see Figure 42 above). Traveling in business and first class typically includes some features offered by top tier status anyway, such as access to priority check-in, priority security lines, and airline lounges.

Some features remain exclusive, such as upgrading our cabin class of travel. If our personal travel experience is enhanced by upgrades and upgrade priority, then the exclusive elements of the status feature set can be more attractive.

When playing the flyer point game at an advanced level, we're more likely to find ourselves on reward seats in business or first class on points, ironically, making status much less relevant. There's an alternate route to those travel benefits through prudent use of our supercharged flyer points.

Furthermore, favoring reward choice over status, can shift our focus onto generic credits cards. We can still elevate our Earn Rate on cash spend through sign-up bonuses and earning generic points on our purchases and then transfer our card points to one of our chosen airline loyalty programs just as needed.

Some credit cards can also provide an alternate route to lounge access. They include memberships of domestic and international lounge networks, including their own branded lounges, such as the Centurion Lounges of American Express, and independent lounge networks, such as Priority Pass. Otherwise, we can buy annual lounge access or pay per visit.

Take outs: do we actually need status? Spoiler alert - the answer is arguably no, well, at least not without a compelling reason. Yes, status is likely to be more relevant to members with a high spend on air travel. Not only will they be able to attain and retain the highest level of status tier to enjoy the full feature set, they will also be able to entertain the associated benefits on a regular or frequent basis.

Very frequent flyers may even be able to attain and maintain status across more than one airline loyalty program to enjoy both the benefits of status and program diversity.

Status features are also pitched at those members who seek to upgrade their cabin class. These members can include those traveling for work whose employer has a policy of paying for travel in economy-coach, leaving the employee to leverage their status and points to fly in a premium cabin through upgrades.

Status is also likely to be more relevant to those members who favor redeeming their points for economy-coach. This is because economy-coach reward seats are relatively easier to find and status tier features, such as priority check-in and lounge access can be enjoyed when flying in economy-coach, depending upon our status tier and program.

But we've already explored alternate routes to many of the travel benefits offered by status. Ditching the conventional and slavish devotion to the status hamster wheel can be liberating because we are released to explore the full scope of reward opportunities and the various strengths and sweet spots of other programs.

POINT BUSTER

Personally, if I was still fixated on status, I would find it much harder to release the full potential of my own flyer points, given my particular personal travel goals, because limited program diversity can negatively impact reward choice. Given that I travel mostly business or first class anyway, the overall value of status is simply not that compelling.

Ideally, if we can have **both** status and flexibility, happy days. But it pays for each of us to make our own fully informed personal choice and not ***presume*** that status is necessary.

JUST LIVE IT: unpack elite status

(Imperial Fora, Rome)

Success - Frankfurt to Rome
Lufthansa Business Class
(avianca life**miles**)

Spin

We all face the ongoing decision of whether to save or redeem our points at any point in time. Choosing more rewards lowers points per reward. That can dilute redeemed value, because richer Target Rewards typically require more points. Choosing fewer rewards increases flexibility, but delivers less reward. We can be rewards poor and sit outside the circle of rewards in the POINT BUSTER (see Figure 43).

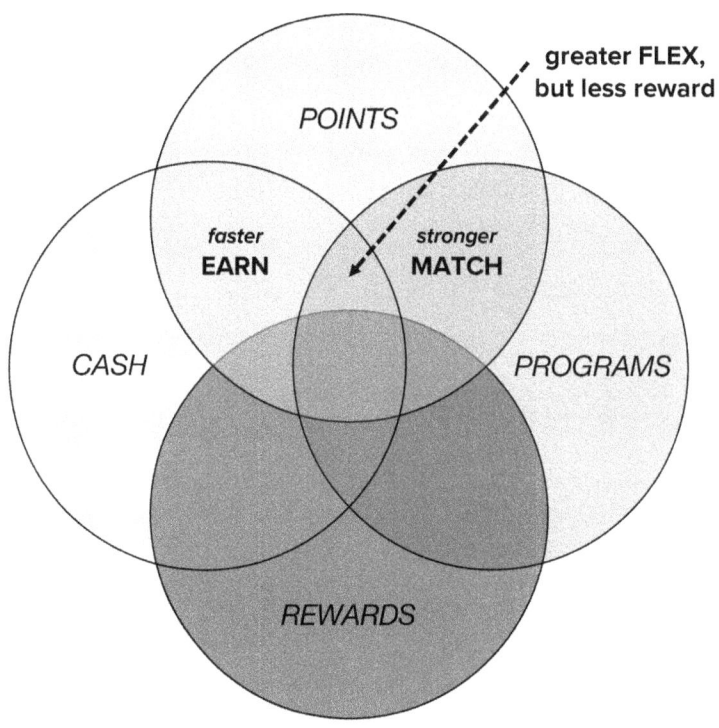

Figure 43: Greater FLEX, but less reward

POINT BUSTER

We can set the balance to suit our individual circumstances by controlling the turnover of our rewards, thus our redemptions over time. Let's explore the flyer point game as a system in motion (see Figure 44).

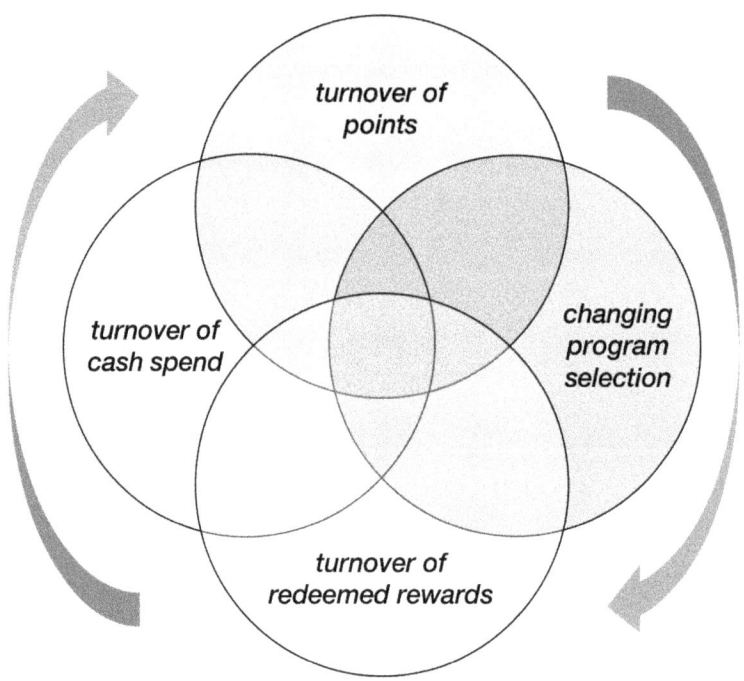

Figure 44: The POINT BUSTER is a system in motion

Spin: the system spins over time. Think one of those fidget toys with four circular wings. We press the middle button to make it rotate.

The cash spent earning points ultimately fuels the speed of spin. But it's not just the amount of cash that matters, but also how much over time.

Spending USD1,000 in one month is twelve times more than USD1,000 in one year. And then it's the turnover of cash spend in combination with Earn Rate that drives total points and thereby kick starts the whole rig into motion.

The initial outcome is seen as growth in total number of points. But that combination of cash spent and average Earn Rate also impacts the ongoing spin, the speed of the earn and redeem cycle, thus turnover of points and rewards over time.

Hoard or burn: we can control the spin to determine the balance between spinning the rig too slowly and too fast. At one extreme, players can be hoarders, endlessly saving points, but not redeeming them and thereby missing out on reward opportunities.

At the other extreme, players can be burners, earning and redeeming points so quickly that they compromise the potential power endowed by higher point totals to deliver greater flexibility and redeemed value.

Dynamics: spoiler alert – there is a complex dynamic system hiding in the heart of the flyer point game. It's complex because different factors impact each other.

It's dynamic because all of those factors are shifting over time as we earn out points, assign them to program accounts, and then redeem them. Ideally, we want to re-stock our points as they are redeemed.

Control: we have several ways to take control of our points and rewards. Firstly, we need a kick starter number of points, enough to meet our redemption goals and diversify our program accounts. Think the cash float in a shop till at the start of trading day or cash in our wallets at the start of a trip.

Secondly, we need to earn enough points over time. The points need to be earned before they can be redeemed. And then they need to be re-stocked for the cycle to be repeated.

Thirdly, with sufficient points, we can aim to match and batch them to our redemption goals, whilst delivering relatively high redeemed value.

Let's consider how to control the spin of the system. Imagine fueling up a car. Without a refill, the gas runs out and the car stops. Imagine each of our chosen airline loyalty program accounts as a tank. We fill each tank with points at a certain rate over time.

A well filled tank has sufficient points to redeem for our goal reward. If needed, we can shift a batch of points from a generic credit card account to top up any given tank as needed.

Making a redemption reduces the volume in the tank, but refilling the tank over time can match our next redemption goal after that.

We can also manage how points are allocated between airline loyalty accounts to afford better Odds at finding reward seats when the time comes to redeem our points.

In practice, the action shifts from one account to another. We can stop filling one of our tanks and start to fill another or otherwise change the relative rates of inflow into our tanks.

Given sufficient points in our generic credit card account, we can be very responsive to opportunities that can arise to redeem points in any program allied to our card product and transfer a batch of points just when required.

Hacks: let's explore just a few ways to control the speed of spin in the POINT BUSTER. Firstly, think faster earn. We can always seek to pump up that proportion of the turnover of our everyday cash spend that earns points. Airline loyalty programs are trending towards ever expanded opportunities to earn points from our daily spend.

We can also pump up our turnover of points by harnessing events, which are relatively rare, but offer relatively higher Earn Rates, as explored earlier in chapter JUICE.

Thus, holders of the Bilt Mastercard have been able to transfer their Bilt Rewards points during occasional Rent Day promotions with transfer bonuses of up to 150 percent, for example, to Emirates Skywards and Air Canada Aeroplan.

Secondly, think stronger match. Adjusting our portfolio to address the challenge of reward seat availability can help to maintain the momentum endowed in the speed of spin kick started by our cash spend and Earn Rate.

Luckily, a speedier spin has the positive impact of reducing the risk of program changes to the required number of points for a given redemption occurring in the time that it takes for us to accrue sufficient points to meet our redemption goals.

Thirdly, think smarter search. We can refine our portfolio of points by taking advantage of positive changes in airline loyalty programs, such as new airline partners, so opening up additional options to redeem our points. We can rebalance our program portfolio over time.

Recently, Alaska Airlines acquired Hawaiian Airlines and also became part of the **one**world airline alliance, whilst Virgin Atlantic became part of the SkyTeam airline alliance.

Fourthly, think wealthier redeem. We can take advantage of periodic promotions featuring a discount, such as those offered by Air France-KLM Flying Blue.

Similarly, Singapore Airlines KrisFlyer has regular Spontaneous Escapes promotions, which are typically released mid-month for flights for the following month. These offer selected routes for less miles, albeit with more restricted terms than the refundable Saver Awards.

Objectivity: even with a tidy number of points in a well-balanced portfolio, we can still face an odd psychological barrier. Some players become attached to the points themselves and resolutely reluctant to redeem them. The speed of spin then slows or stops completely. Their turnover of rewards is now limiting their gameplay.

The obvious answer is to keep our focus on our overall performance, the game isn't won by the players with the highest total number of points, rather by those who satisfy their individual goals and enjoy travel rich reward. And that means nurturing our turnover of rewards.

Finally, some players consider hoarding their points for their future retirement. But the trend is for programs to increase the required number of points for a given reward over time. The redeemed value of hoarded points is potentially depreciating.

The impact is greater the longer the points are kept. A reward seat that requires 100,000 today, will cost 144,000 points at some time in the future, after two devaluations of 20 percent. There is also the risk that the program switches to dynamic pricing of rewards, thus completely changing the goalposts.

That said, a thorough analysis would also need to take into account any inflation in the cost of paid airfares, since redeemed value is objectively calculated against the cost of the equivalent retail price of the reward seat.

The reality is that the airline loyalty program universe is so changeable that the goal posts shift very fast. Current trends include minimum cash spend to attain given status tiers and dynamic pricing of reward seats.

It's hard to plan beyond the relatively short term with any certainty. Arguably, players who are flexible, adaptable, and balance the turnover of their points and rewards will find themselves at an advantage.

Take outs: we can seek to control the turnover of our cash spend that earns points, our points totals, our selection of programs, and redemption of rewards over time.

The amount of our spend combined with our average Earn Rate creates the spin that puts the system into motion. Initially we stock up on points, and then aim to redeem and restock them at rates that satisfy our ongoing travel goals. We can thereby match our turnover of rewards to the cycle of earning and restocking our points in a way that's sustainable.

We can adjust our portfolio of programs not just to take advantage of their respective strengths and reward availability, but also the inevitable changes to the programs themselves.

Basically, we can balance hoarding and burning our flyer points and assume control of the dynamics of the system. There's one final hurdle. Our perceptions of value.

JUST LIVE IT: balance the burn

POINT BUSTER

(Pantheon, Rome)

EXPERIENCE HISTORY

Value

Pay-offs in the flyer point game vary greatly. We can be left behind or enjoy travel rich reward. Objective measures of value are crucial to guide our gameplay.

Moreover, rewards offering greater redeemed value tend to be harder to find. We need to take control of that, or risk inadvertently accepting better Odds of success, but less value.

When we don't relate our reward back to our cash spend, we're sitting outside of the circle of cash in the POINT BUSTER (see Figure 45).

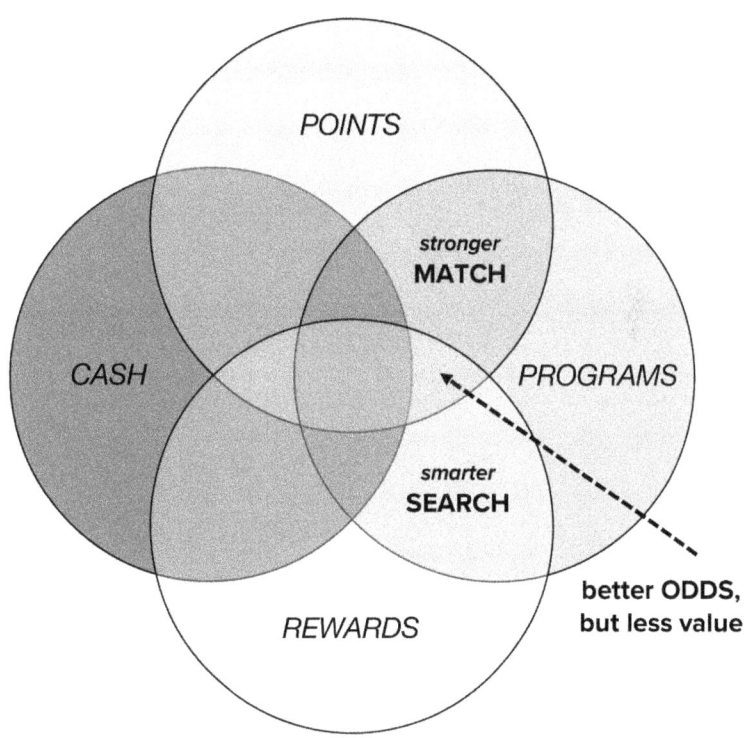

Figure 45: Better ODDS, but less value

POINT BUSTER

Value: we've already discussed the six seductive facets of flyer points in chapter WIN. But there's another challenge, our potentially conflicting perceptions of value.

There are three classic aspects to a product or service: the features, their attendant benefits, and then the value of each, as applicable to a given customer.

Let's consider just one of my personal favorite features of a business class reward, namely, a lie-flat seat. The benefit is that it's much easier to sleep. The value is arriving at my destination feeling relaxed and refreshed.

We can approach value in two ways, either defined exactly and mathematically, or not. Sometimes we can easily assess benefits in cash terms, for example, calculating the redeemed value of our flyer points offered by a given reward option.

But sometimes that's not so easily done. A business class reward seat can include lounge benefits, such as a refreshing shower, which can feel great and lead to a sense of satisfaction, but be hard to quantify in dollar terms.

Satisfaction: let's chart our Pay-off against our personal sense of satisfaction. The horizontal axis is the mathematically defined Pay-off. The vertical axis is a measure of how an individual can perceive their travel experience.

For ease and convenience, I've defined that as satisfaction. It's a ranking of an individual's emotional response.

I've very simply assigned ratings of low and high. When somebody gets what they want, they feel good and experience high satisfaction. When they don't, they feel low satisfaction. I've also ranked Pay-off very simply as low and high. That generates four quadrants on the chart (see Figure 46).

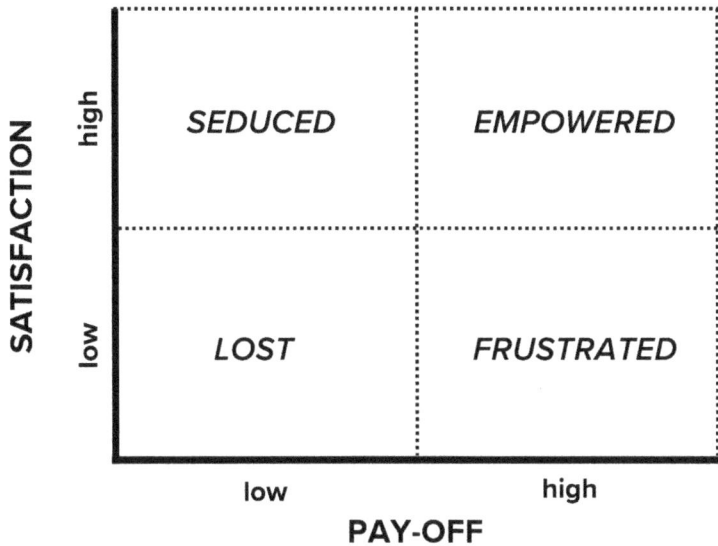

Figure 46: We can balance Pay-off with satisfaction

If our efforts in the flyer point game misfire, a low Pay-off combines with low satisfaction. Arguably, we are lost. By contrast, if a high Pay-off combines with a high sense of satisfaction, we are empowered.

A high sense of satisfaction can combine with a lowly Pay-off, by ignoring the math and thereby using our points inefficiently. Although we're feeling great, we've potentially been seduced by points.

That leaves the combination of a high Pay-off, but low satisfaction. We can redeem for rewards, which use our points efficiently, but they don't satisfy us for some reason. Perhaps we can redeem for business class reward seats, but only to our second-choice destination. That can leave us frustrated.

The better our gameplay, the more open the door to the empowered quadrant, in which we score a great Pay-off and feel satisfied at the same time. I personally favor redeeming my points for longer flights in a premium cabin class. I feel satisfied, whilst still enjoying a great Pay-off.

Subjective value: now let's consider some commonly held concepts and perceptions of value. I've simply demarcated these into subjective and objective, and then further classified them by earn, redeem, and reward (see Figure 47).

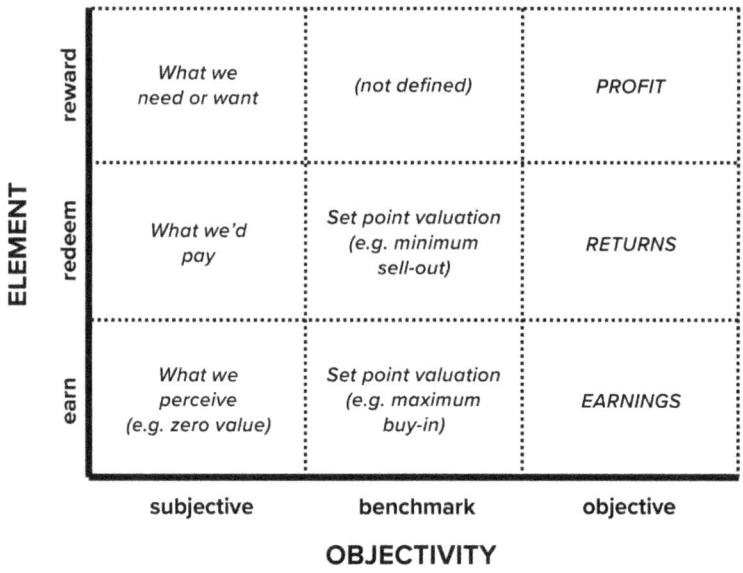

Figure 47: Contrasting approaches to value

Subjective concepts of value are those unique to an individual or folk of similar perception. Thus, some program members perceive that they earned their points for nothing, their points were free and thereby have no intrinsic value.

They believe that points were giveaway items. Any rewards are a bonus. But points aren't free. We, or our employers, have paid for them either directly or indirectly. If we fall into the trap of undervaluing our points or redeemed reward, then we run the risk of missing out on more bang for buck.

Some take the entirely subjective position of valuing their points based upon the cash they would be willing to pay for the ticket, or against a personal budget, as already introduced in chapter POINTS.

I've been planning to go from Sydney to Johannesburg. Imagine that my budget for that flight was USD850, just enough for a one-way economy-coach retail airfare. Great, if I can find reward seats, should I feel as though I can save that cash, but only if I spend the points? Does that mean that the points spent are only worth the cash saved?

But hold on, I'm not gaining cash, but rather product when I redeem my points. If I choose a better product, a business class reward seat, over a lesser product, an economy-coach class reward seat, in my mind I would still have only saved my subjectively nominated budget.

Moreover, by that logic I would have effectively lowered the value of my flyer points, because the business class reward requires more points for the same notional cash saved. That's despite getting more product, thus more per point and thereby more bang for original buck spent. That seems illogical.

A third subjective perception arises when players focus on what they need or want. A friend had used his points to fly his daughter in economy-coach to travel to college believing that he was saving cash. The flights were cheap to purchase, so the redeemed value of his points was relatively very low.

His sense of meeting an immediate need had dictated his perception of value. But after our debrief, he switched his focus and booked his very first business class reward seats to treat his wife on their upcoming overseas vacation. He unlocked far more bang for buck.

Objective value: in comparison to the subjective perceptions of individuals, objective concepts of value are mathematically exact and can be repeated. Two program members would come up with exactly the same result, when they apply the same mathematical method. That result can then inform personal choice.

Obviously, the focus in this book is an objective approach. Earn Rate measures value when earning points and Returns measures value when redeeming points.

A given combination of those two delivers a potential Profit score. That is realized given reward availability to become our Pay-off.

Our objective method exposes the extraordinary variation in Pay-offs and cool patterns hiding in the numbers that can help us to elevate our gameplay. Thus, it reveals the implicit power of our strategic boosters and exposes the inter-relationships between the parts in the underlying system. It thereby finally clears a path for us to supercharge our flyer points.

Benchmark valuations: people typically want to know how much their points are worth, so some websites and travel blogs publish point valuations. These are quoted in US Cents or other cash currency per point and fixed at the one-size-fits-all figure. In practice the proposed point valuations for a given airline loyalty program are fairly consistent from blog to blog.

I've personally chosen to categorize such valuations as **benchmarks**. That's because such valuations can guide some yes or no choices, which players can face in the flyer point game.

I've also chosen to define these as partly objective because they are partly data derived by taking into account the Returns and other factors that typify a given program.

They are partly subjective because each takes a different approach and can vary based upon factors that aren't always clearly defined. They are also not reproducible by any player, unlike an objective measure.

The good news is that benchmark valuations can potentially save us from making a rookie error of undervaluing our saved points. Imagine a benchmark valuation of USD15 per 1000 points (or 1.5 US Cents per point). A redemption offering Returns below the benchmark, say USD5 per 1000 points for a hotel booking is ill-advised.

Any given reward offering Returns above the benchmark is acceptable. Furthermore, the higher the Returns above the benchmark, the more confident that we can feel that we are releasing relatively good value, when redeeming our flyer points. We can also derive our own target for redeemed value based upon a published benchmark, for example, by simply doubling it from USD15 to USD30 per 1000 points.

Benchmark valuations can also guide a decision to buy points by setting both a maximum buy-in cash price and a minimum sell-out redeemed value per point. I've charted that to show the range of acceptable combinations (see Figure 48).

POINT BUSTER

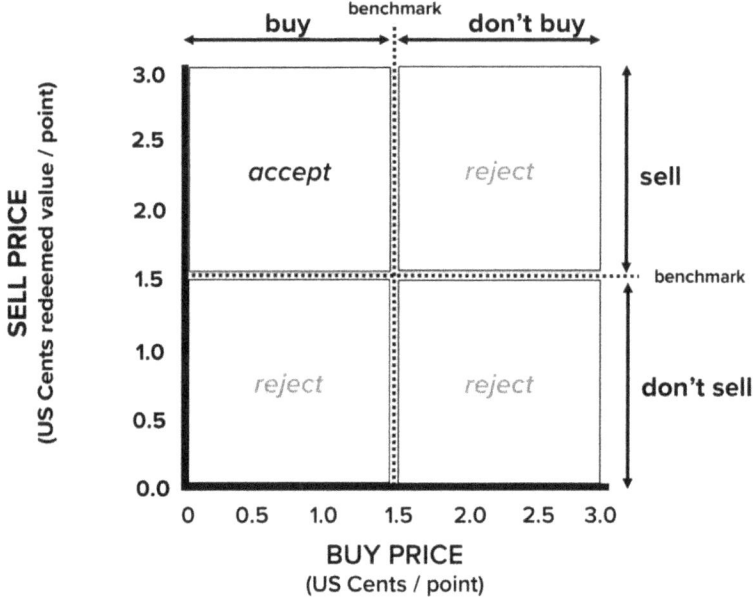

Figure 48: Benchmarking for buy and sell (redeem) options

The horizontal axis represents the buy price and the vertical axis the sell price. There is a quadrant of acceptable combinations wherein the sell exceeds the buy price.

Catch: let's sanity check the method. I've redrawn the buy and sell scenario on a chart similar to a Profit table, only this time it's focused upon flipping cash to redeemed value, since we're buying points rather than earning them.

I've rewritten the benchmark buy price as a Purchase Rate. That's the number of points purchased per dollar, in this case 100 divided by 1.5, thus 66.7 points per USD. Now we aim to accept Purchase Rates above that benchmark and redeem our points above the benchmark sell price of USD15 redeemed value per 1000 points (see Figure 49).

PAY-OFF

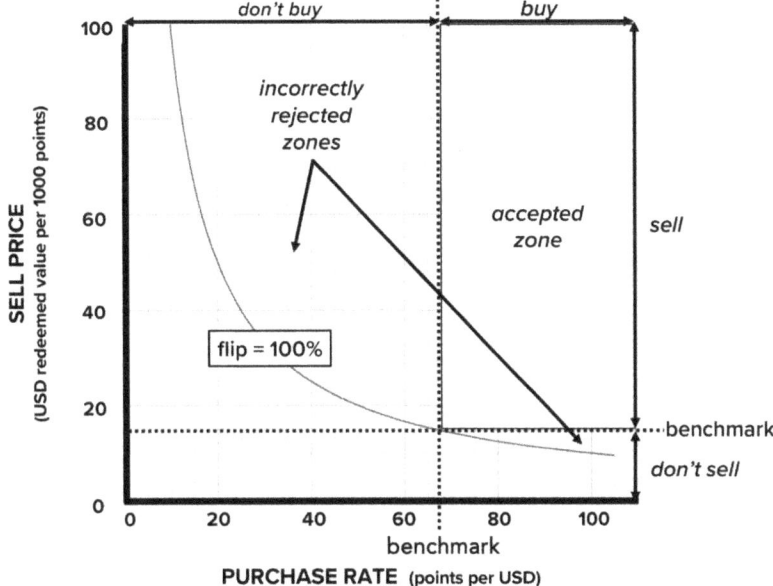

Figure 49: Benchmarking is inefficient

The accepted zone of buy and sell combinations is now a rectangle to the upper right of the chart. I've added a curve joining combinations of Purchase Rate and sell price that deliver a 100 percent flip from cash to redeemed value.

We need to be to the right and above that curve, where the redeemed value received is greater than the cash expended, thus above 100 percent.

The chart shows that whereas the benchmarking method correctly identifies some combinations of Purchase Rate and sell price above the 100 percent flip curve, it also incorrectly rejects many others. It does work, but it's inefficient.

There's another limitation. Benchmark valuations bypass the huge variation that exists in Earn Rate. Let's illustrate that by choosing a benchmark valuation of USD15 redeemed value per 1000 points (US Cents 1.5 per point).

POINT BUSTER

Combining that benchmark valuation with an Earn Rate of 5 points per USD delivers a Profit score of 7.5 percent, but coupled with an Earn Rate of 20 points per USD it delivers a Profit score of 30 percent, and with an Earn Rate of 66.7 points per USD delivers a Profit score of 100 percent, and so forth.

Benchmark valuations, are a one-size-fits-all approach. They tell us nothing about our Profit score, or Pay-off, if we successfully redeem our flyer points.

Let's consider another hypothetical case. Imagine a credit card, that earns points at a basic Earn Rate of 1 point per USD. Applying the benchmark valuation cited above delivers a Profit score of just 1.5 percent.

That equates to receiving 1.5 US Cents back in redeemed value for each dollar spent on the card, without factoring in any transaction and annual fees. Even relaxing that Earn Rate to 3 points per USD only delivers a Profit score of 4.5 percent.

If we used such a benchmark valuation to assess what we get back from our ongoing credit card flyer point earn for our loyal spend, we might decide it just wasn't worthwhile.

Of course, we can get more back simply by targeting rewards with relatively higher Returns. We can also amass points from credit card sign up and retention bonuses, not just the applicable base earning rate.

Now let's explore an example of how benchmark valuations can incur problematic results. I researched redeeming British Airways Club points, called Avios, on partner airline Iberia for a one-way business class seat from Miami to Madrid. In some scenarios, Avios buck the trend by offering relatively high redeemed value in small batches.

There were several pricing options of Avios and a cash co-payment. I ran the numbers for each of the six combinations (see Figure 50).

REWARD (retail value USD3023)		Returns USD/ 1000 Avios	cost estimate of reward (USD) based upon benchmark valuation*				
Avios	cash copayment USD		USD11/ 1000 Avios	USD13/ 1000 Avios	USD17/ 1000 Avios	USD18/ 1000 Avios	USD19/ 1000 Avios
42,500	133	68	601	686	856	898	941
36,150	229	77	627	699	844	880	916
27,650	341	97	645	700	811	839	866
21,250	454	121	688	730	815	837	858
14,900	567	165	731	761	820	835	850
8500	681	275	775	792	826	834	843

*[(number of Avios) x (benchmark valuation)] + cash copayment

Figure 50: Benchmarking can be misleading

The Returns stepped up from worst to best as Avios were lessened and cash co-payments increased. The least was USD68 per 1000 Avios and the best USD275 per 1000 Avios.

For comparison, I chose a benchmark valuation of USD13 per 1000 Avios, typical of some travel blogs. I used that to identify the combination of least cost and thereby the most valuable. I simply multiplied the number of Avios by the benchmark valuation and added the cash co-payment for each combination.

Problematically, the benchmark valuation method ranks the combinations in exactly the reverse order than that derived from our objective valuation based upon Returns.

POINT BUSTER

When I lowered the benchmark value to USD11 per 1000 Avios, the ranking didn't change. But when I increased the benchmark valuation to USD18 per 1000 Avios or more, the ranking flipped and aligned with that of our objective method.

The numbers will differ according to the chosen example, but this case study demonstrates that the result we derive can be highly sensitive to the benchmark valuation that we choose. In this particular scenario, the initial benchmark valuation quite simply underestimated the value of Avios.

That benchmark valuation would have misdirected us away from the highest redeemed value, delivered by the sixth combination, in favor of the lowest, delivered by the first. The highest possible redeemed value was also over 20 times more than the benchmark valuation itself. Clearly, we can't be guided solely by such benchmark valuations in our gameplay.

Take outs: in the flyer point game we are rewarded with product not cash. But we can still put a value on that product to help us to measure our reward. We can do that objectively, by using the retail price of the product. That exposes that we can enjoy vastly different reward for the same spend.

Some players value their reward subjectively. They can focus on perceptions of cash saved, but miss the opportunity to satisfy their travel goals ***and*** get more product for their original cash spend. They risk not getting more bang for buck.

It's tempting to put a fixed valuation on our flyer points. In some scenarios, this can save us from undervaluing our points, but we also need to consider that our points are highly dynamic.

They don't have fixed values and their redeemed values vary hugely. Our Pay-off depends both upon how easily we earn our points **and** how much redeemed value they release.

Ideally, we can leverage our gameplay to satisfy our travel goals and get relatively great bang for buck, basically more travel rich reward for the same loyal spend.

JUST LIVE IT: unveil true value

(Suvarnabhumi International Airport, Bangkok)

TRAVEL POOR TO RICH

POINT BUSTER

(Galleria Vittorio Emanuele II, Milan)

EMPOWER EVERYDAY SPEND

SUPERCHARGED

We started with two imaginary customers, who each spent USD1000 in a shop. One received the reward of a credit voucher for just USD5 and the other for up to USD5000 off the retail price of a future purchase. That illustrates in simple terms, what can happen playing the flyer point game.

That shouldn't sound as extraordinary as it once did. Flyer points can deliver widely different bang for buck. It's time to fuse all of the parts captured in the POINT BUSTER to seize opportunities to supercharge our flyer points (see Figure 51).

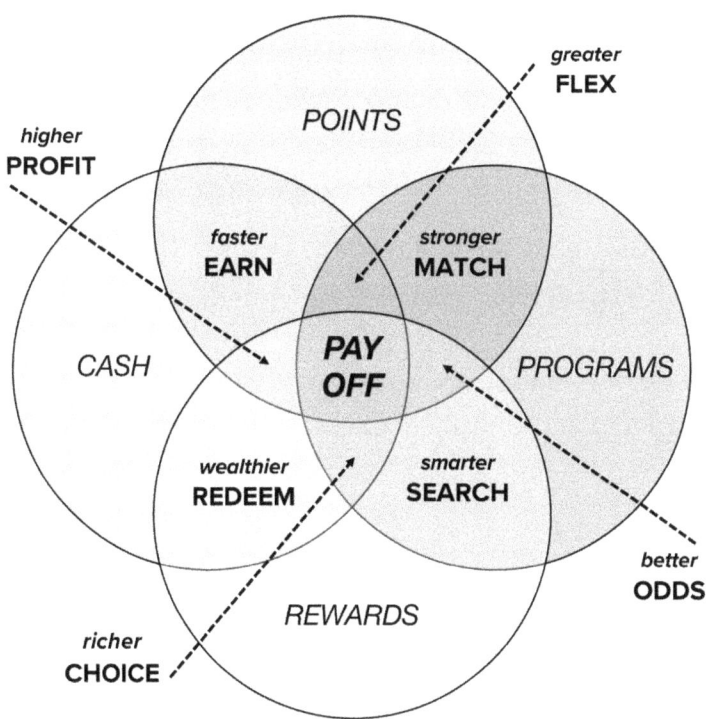

Figure 51: The POINT BUSTER

The POINT BUSTER

Cash: we can empower everyday spend. Cash fuels the system. Spending money with airlines and other partners of any given airline loyalty program earns flyer points.

Points: we can fortify flyer points. They are simply loyalty tokens, bridging cash spend to a reward. Flyer points are typically unique to a given airline loyalty program. They are highly dynamic, since they typically unlock vastly varying travel rich reward for our cash spend earning points.

Programs: we can play the programs. They are based upon potentially profitable marketing models, which monetize loyalty. They are designed to lock in our business with the program's parent airline and a wide range of partners, whilst scooping up coin. Whilst broadly similar, individual programs can offer strengths and sweet spots of potential advantage to our gameplay.

Rewards: we can reap more reward. Many different rewards are offered, depending upon the given airline loyalty program. Seats on a plane typically offer the most redeemed value for our points, especially Award Seats and competitively priced Dynamic Rewards. These Target Rewards can be in limited supply and thereby harder to find.

Earn: we can propel a faster earn with six proven actions. The number of points earned per dollar varies greatly. The combination of our spend and Earn Rate drives our points totals.

Match: we can secure a stronger match with six proven actions. We match points to programs as they are earned, although points can sometimes be exchanged. Program strengths can help to deliver our redemption goals and direct our program selection. Program diversity can also generate more search Options for when the time comes to redeem our points.

Search: we can master a smarter search with six proven actions. Our Target Rewards can be limited in availability and harder to find. The trick is to broaden our search and hone our skills to find those, which are available, but waiting to be found.

Redeem: we can enrich a wealthier redeem with six proven actions. Flyer points only release their potential, when they are redeemed for a reward and then their redeemed value varies greatly. Target Rewards typically unlock the most value. Those reward seats in premium cabin classes can also offer a more comfortable travel experience.

Flex: we can combine the actions for a faster earn and stronger match to boost greater flexibility. Flyer points become more empowered in higher numbers, because Target Rewards in premium cabins and on longer flights cost relatively more points. Moreover, the more points saved, the more that we can spread them across multiple programs to access their strengths and to outwit limited Target Reward availability.

Odds: we can combine the actions for a stronger match and smarter search to boost greater Odds of successfully finding Target Rewards.

The trick is to plan ahead for more flight search Options and also increase our capacity to find reward seats. The boost is based upon the way that combinations escalate exponentially when we search across increasing numbers of search Options.

Choice: we can combine the actions for a smarter search and a wealthier redeem to boost richer Choice. This can reveal more rewards to choose from, thereby increasing the likelihood of satisfying our travel goals, whilst also unlocking relatively higher redeemed value.

Profit: we can combine the actions for a faster earn and a wealthier redeem to boost higher Profit. Earn Rates multiply Returns to generate our Profit score. Our Profit becomes our Pay-off when we reveal available reward seats.

Pay-off: we can expose vastly different bang for buck rewarded for the same cash spend by calculating Pay-offs. These vary hugely and can guide our end-to-end gameplay.

Because all of the parts of the flyer point game are interlinked, our Pay-off can be limited when we are points poor, or programs poor, or rewards poor, or fail to relate value back to our cash spend,

Juice: we can hunt plentiful points to avoid being points poor. Opportunities to earn more points per dollar can be harder to find. Whereas they require more effort, they can deliver many more points.

Status: we can unpack elite status to avoid being programs poor. Status offers an array of features in return for our loyal business with a given program's parent airline and partners.

But status can lock us into the one program and thereby restrict access to available Target Rewards and the strengths of each program. There are alternative routes to some status features through premium travel and certain credit cards.

Spin: we can balance the burn to avoid being rewards poor, by managing the turnover of our cash spend, points, selection of airline loyalty programs, and rewards.

Cash spent and Earn Rate combine to power up the whole rig and determine its spin, the least time taken from when a point is earned until it's redeemed. Thereafter, we can balance hoarding points for fewer, or burning points for more reward redemptions, whilst seeking richer redeemed value for our points. We can balance points redeemed with points earned and restocked for a sustainable approach to our gameplay.

Value: we can unveil true value to avoid missing opportunities to unlock more bang for buck. Objective measures of value can be calculated and applied consistently by anyone. They also expose the power of the math to guide our gameplay.

Subjective approaches to value include the cash that an individual would be prepared to pay for a reward and perceptions of potential cash saved against a personal budget. These can guide reward choice, but steer us away from options offering more bang for buck.

Benchmark valuations of points can guide basic choices, such as the minimum redeemed value at which to redeem our flyer points. But since flyer points do not have fixed values, benchmark valuations alone are insufficient to inform our gameplay beyond a basic level.

POINT BUSTER

(Wet Tropics World Heritage Area – Far North Queensland)
EXPERIENCE NATURE

Energize the Supercharge

Let's recap the five ways to supercharge our points to seek travel richer reward. Firstly, we can charge up our points by seizing opportunity to earn them at higher Earn Rates. Whereas one transaction can offer an Earn Rate of 1 point or less per USD, another can deliver 10 points per USD and another 100 points or more per USD, and so forth.

Individual points earned at different rates, have the capacity to deliver vastly different Profit scores and realized Pay-offs, when redeemed for a reward.

Secondly, we can charge up our points by how we group them together. Each individual point becomes more powerful when grouped in ever higher numbers of points.

Thirdly, we can charge up our points by how effectively that we assign them across different program accounts, thus potentially generating more flight search Options for when the time comes to redeem our points for our goal reward.

A point in a program account offering a sweet spot meeting our travel goals is more powerful than a point that isn't. A point that can be transferred to another program account or sits in a portfolio of multiple program accounts is inherently more powerful than a point sitting in a portfolio of just one program.

Fourthly, we can charge up our points by increasing our capacity to redeem them. Any improvement in our search skills can increase our Chances of finding available Target Rewards waiting to be found. A point endowing more Options and greater Chances can elevate our Odds of successfully finding our Target Rewards.

Fifthly, we can charge up our points by seizing opportunity to redeem them for rewards of greater redeemed value. The higher the Returns, the greater the realized redeemed value of any given point.

Our points can end up with zero or high charge or any charge in between. To illustrate the concept of variable charge of flyer points very simply, let's consider just a couple of the many possible permutations of the ways in which individual flyer points can be charged.

Imagine that we earn Point A at a relatively slow Earn Rate of 1 point per USD. This point ends up in an account with limited total points. It sits in a portfolio of just one program account and thus offers only weak Options to search out Target Rewards (see Figure 52).

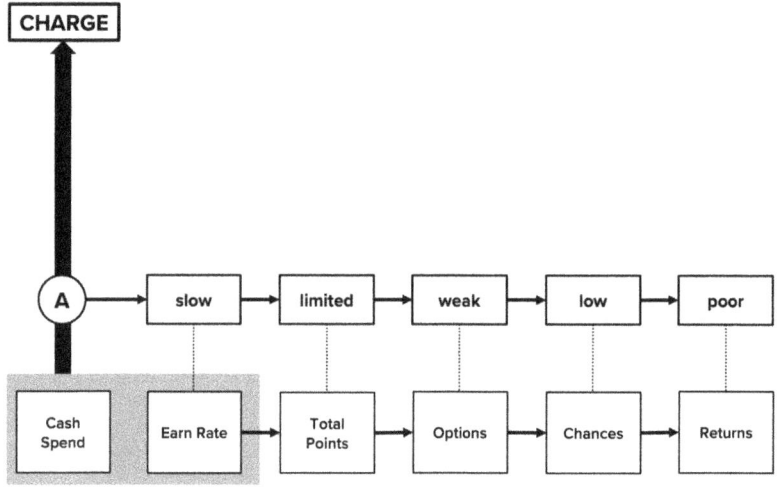

Figure 52: Point A has a trickling charge

Point A's capacity to elevate our Chances of finding Target Rewards is low. Those Options and Chances do little to elevate our overall Odds of successfully finding our goal Target Rewards.

Point A is likely to end up offering poor Returns depending upon how it is redeemed. Its charge is just a trickle. The redeemed value is meagre compared with the original cash spend. This point potentially delivers a relatively low Pay-off.

Now imagine that we earn Point B at a fast Earn Rate of 50 points per USD. This point ends up joining sufficient other points to form a plentiful supply of total points.

Point B can sit within a portfolio of multiple program accounts, so contributing to a strong scope of Options when searching for Target Rewards. This point offers high Chances of finding a range of rewards (see Figure 53).

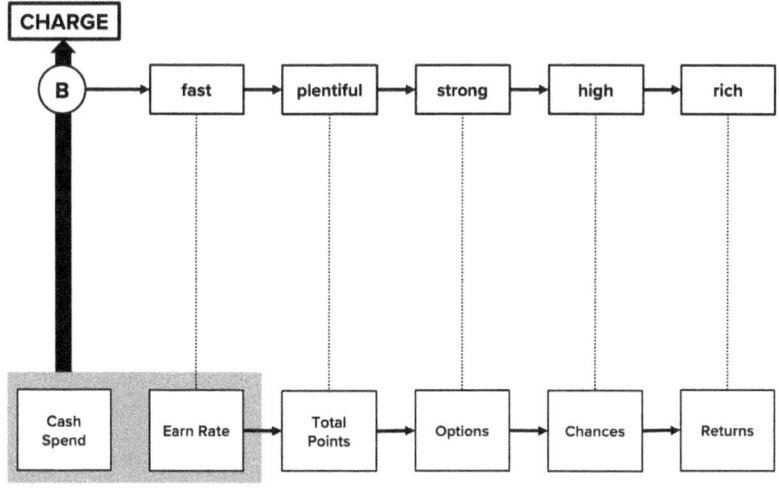

Figure 53: Point B has a sizzling charge

Those Options and Chances can greatly boost our overall Odds of successfully securing our goal Target Rewards. Point B ends up offering rich Returns depending on how it is redeemed. The redeemed value is potentially much greater than the original cash spend. Point B is supercharged. It has the potential capacity to deliver a relatively high Pay-off

In reality different points in our stash can carry completely different charge. Some can have low charge, others are supercharged, and yet others have a charge which lies somewhere in between. Pay-offs thereby vary greatly when we redeem different points.

Basically, unleashing superior bang for buck depends upon seizing opportunities to earn and redeem our points, and our flyer point gameplay. We can energize the supercharge.

Outwit the Complex

The stark variation in Pay-offs arises because there's a complex dynamic system at the core of the flyer point game. Basically, the component parts are all either directly or indirectly interconnected. Positive impacts can accelerate and negative impacts can disempower our gameplay.

Let's explore just one small chunk of the underlying system. I've created a chart to illustrate the interplay between the various factors that impact the relationships between our total points, Returns, and Odds of success.

Solid arrows indicate positive impacts and dashed arrows negative impacts. A negative impact undermines any downstream positive impacts. Thus, higher Returns lower reward availability, thereby our Chances, and thereby Odds of success (see Figure 54).

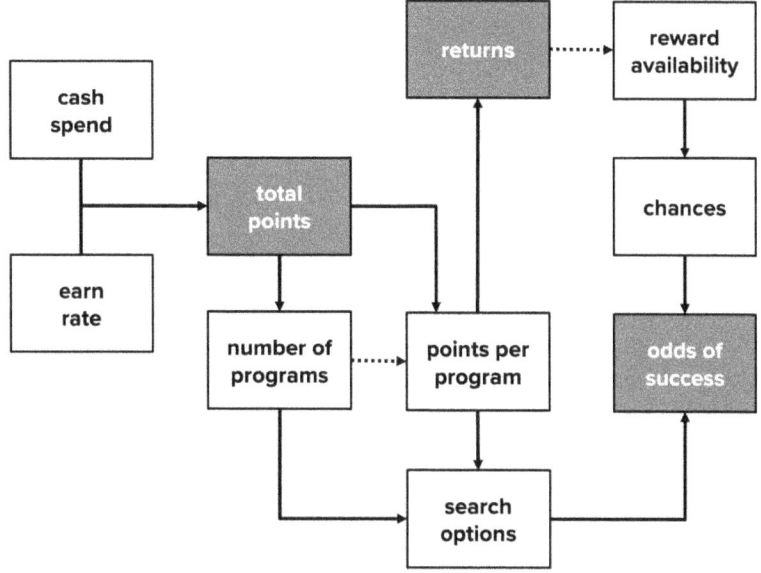

Figure 54: Interplay between total points, Returns, and Odds

Cash spend and Earn Rate drive total points. Then higher points totals drive greater flexibility by creating the opportunity to increase the number of programs and points per program in our portfolio.

The number of programs negatively impacts points per program because a given total number of points needs to be spread over more programs.

A higher total number of points total in any given program typically extends our choice of rewards offering ever greater Returns. That's simply because more valuable Target Rewards tend to require higher numbers of points.

The catch is that rewards offering greater Returns are typically less available and thereby harder to find. Higher Returns therefore can negatively impact reward availability.

Better Target Reward availability increases our Chances of finding our goal reward whatever our reward search skills, because there are more rewards in play waiting to be found.

Our overall Odds of successfully finding our goal Target Rewards is positively impacted by both our Chances of finding available rewards and the number of search Options that we have generated through how flexibly we've managed our programs and points portfolio.

We can address the two negative impacts. We can balance the number of programs and number of points per program in our portfolio to increase the number of flight search Options and thereby our Odds of success. We can offset the lesser availability of Target Rewards offering relatively higher Returns. We do that by maturing our reward search skills to up our Chances of revealing rewards waiting to be found and by increasing our search Options. Both increase our Odds of success. Addressing these negative impacts is ever more significant as we seek rewards of relatively higher Returns.

Let's consider the practical implications. Firstly, having sufficient points is potentially critical for redeeming rewards of increasing Returns. It's also the key to diversifying our points and programs portfolio to deliver the extra flight search Options required to offset declining Odds of successfully finding more valuable rewards, which are less available and harder to find.

Secondly, the flexibility in our approach is crucial. We can mature our portfolio of points and programs, potentially backed by one or more generic credit cards, because they afford the facility to transfer points as required.

Thirdly, we're less likely to attain relatively higher Returns without seeking to control the relationships between total points, flight search Options, Chances, and Odds of success.

Fourthly, this is a very different approach to fixating upon point valuations alone. When we're only focused on one or two factors and consider them in isolation, we risk failing to unlock more bang for buck from our points.

Points aren't a cash currency. They don't typically have fixed values. They can be earned at vastly different rates and unlock hugely variable redeemed value. Being overly simple in our approach can misdirect us away from the secrets of the flyer point game hiding in plain sight.

Taking a systems approach can help us to become more certain of finding Target Rewards across a broader range of Returns, improve our Odds of successfully finding rarer Target Rewards offering higher Returns, and increase our ability to take control of the system. Basically, we can seek to outwit the complex.

Gameplay the System

Our choices can limit or liberate our control of those relationships between the parts in the system. That's because each of our actions can have immediate and downstream impacts. Thus, on the one hand, harnessing an excellent Earn Rate can magnify our point totals with the attendant downstream benefits and extract greater value. But on the other hand, being locked into just the one airline loyalty program can potentially limit our access to reward seats. We can harness a holistic approach to gameplay the system.

POINT BUSTER

(Marina Bay Sands from the Fullerton Bay Hotel, Singapore)

Success - Singapore to London
Singapore Airlines First Class Suites
(Singapore Airlines KrisFlyer)

Empower Cash Spend

Our everyday cash spend on stuff earning points is the fuel that drives the system. Some of us can harness huge cash spend, for example those with a handy turnover of cash coursing through their business. But others are relatively limited by the amount of cash flow that they spend with program airlines and partners. In either case, the four strategic boosters of crafting greater Flex, generating better Odds, driving richer Choice and unlocking greater Profit can be combined to unleash more travel rich reward. We can empower cash spend.

Electrify the Positive

The mostly positive relationships between the parts in the system create the opportunity to boost our gameplay. Thus, actions increasing both cash spend and Earn Rate accelerate numbers of points. Actions increasing numbers of points and a stronger portfolio accelerate flexibility. Actions increasing search Options and Chances of finding Target Rewards accelerate Odds of success. Actions increasing both Earn Rate and Returns accelerate Profit score, and so forth. We can electrify the positive.

Neutralize the Negative

We can overcome those relationships between the parts in the system, which limit our gameplay. Thus, sheer numbers of points can jolt us out of being points limited, when seeking greater flexibility and redeemed value. We can bypass status or find ways to maintain status that do not impact the diversity of our program portfolio. We can neutralize the negative.

POINT BUSTER

Vitalize the Variation

There is huge variation in both how many points we can earn per dollar and how much redeemed value that we can unlock per point. It's that variation that creates the opportunity to accelerate our Pay-off.

Remarkably, more action goes down at the front end than the back end. The greatest variation I've come across in Earn Rate within the same program is about 300 times. By contrast, the greatest variation, which I've personally experienced for Returns within the same airline loyalty program is about 20 times. Earn Rates can show ten times or greater variation than Returns. Earn Rates can have greater potential to drive our Pay-off than Returns. We can vitalize the variation.

Refresh for flexibility

The system is always changing. The various factors in play, and their respective positive and negative impacts, are fluid over time. Earning opportunities come and go, programs devalue, but add new partners, reward seat availability varies, and so forth. We can plan for and be responsive to change and continually refresh for flexibility.

Ride the Numbers

The simple math-based holistic approach of the POINT BUSTER can always guide our gameplay. Thus, it can inform a counter strategy to outplay the increasing trend for airline loyalty programs to adopt dynamic pricing of rewards. The objective math will always expose whether or not we're being seduced by points.

SUPERCHARGED

Fortunately, we are all everyday spenders and can harness the trend for ever greater opportunities to earn our flyer points through our personal, household, and business cash spend.

Our action power packs and strategic boosters have the potential to supercharge our points and empower our daily spend for travel rich reward. We have the choice to ride the numbers.

JUST LIVE IT: be travel rich

(Port Douglas)

Success - Hong Kong to Cairns
Cathay Pacific Business Class
(Alaska Airlines Mileage Plan)

POINT BUSTER

("The Horse Problem" by Argentinian artist, Claudia Fontes)

UNLEASH ATOMIC POINTS

SHOUT-OUT

My university supervisor, Professor Vladimir Brusic, encouraged me to explore the world of dynamic systems, whilst undergrad tutors Professor Pat Bateson and Professor Nick Davies fostered an interest in animal behavior and the application of game theory to behavioral strategy. High school English teacher, Margaret Melicharova, instilled a passion for the written word.

The idea to capture the gig holistically in a Venn diagram was inspired by one depicting purpose, widely shared online, but attributed to Spaniard Andrés Zuzunaga, director of **Cosmograma** in Barcelona.

Multiple published author Simon Rumney bolstered my confidence to write, business consultant Gary Reynolds advised me to focus on everyday cash spend, and long-term friend Dwaine Laxdal provided invaluable editorial feedback.

My approach differs somewhat to that of some frequent flyer bloggers and commentators, but my background knowledge has been furthered over many years by their countless articles on blog sites and bulletin boards too numerous to hat tip individually.

Gratitude to all airline workers for their overwhelmingly professional and gracious efforts over the decades of enjoyable travel experiences.

I acknowledge the peoples who are the Traditional Custodians of the Land where I live and this book was written and pay respect to their Elders both past and present.

POINT BUSTER

(Tagus River, Lisbon)

DON'T DREAM IT

BIO

Peter approaches the flyer point game uniquely from the perspective of a bio-scientist, drawing upon his experience in strategy theory and behavior, and ecological and genetic systems. He holds Master's degrees from the University of Cambridge and the University of Sydney.

He also draws upon his 30-years of experience as a business consultant to communicate the complex in simple terms. He has developed multimedia marketing and dozens of corporate training programs, across various industries from aviation to telecommunications, and from conservation management to the resources sector. He has prepared feasibility study reports for a number of multi-billion-dollar global engineering projects.

Peter was first introduced to airline loyalty programs nearly 40 years ago by his father, a globetrotting expert in squeezing the system for cheap travel.

Peter then embarked upon the painful learning process to master every aspect of the flyer point game. He lost a whole hire car on his way to Honolulu Airport, when earning his very first flyer points, spilt his predeparture champagne on his initial first-class reward flight from Sydney to London, and mislaid the draft of this entire book by accidentally leaving his laptop computer behind in a hotel room in Madrid.

When not flying around the planet on supercharged flyer points, Peter lives in the Wet Tropics of Queensland, amongst the local wallabies, kookaburras, and ancient rainforest.

POINT BUSTER

(The Alps, northern Italy)

JUST LIVE IT

STEP UP

Continue your point busting adventures through:

www.pointbuster.com

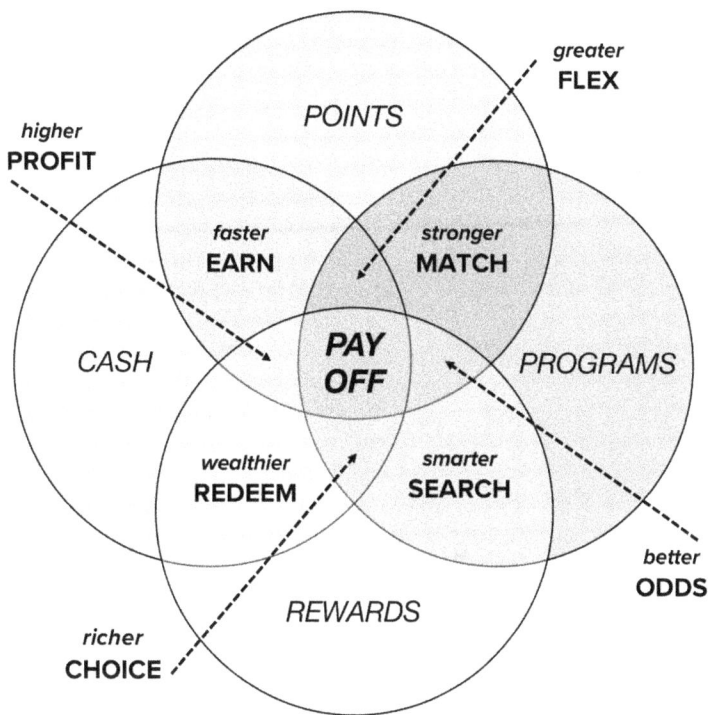

POINT BUSTER

**wildlife search pty limited
2025**

www.ingramcontent.com/pod-product-compliance
Lightning Source LLC
Chambersburg PA
CBHW061206070526
44583CB00025B/3139